CONTROL CHARTS

CONTROL CHARTS

J. MURDOCH

Head of Statistics and Operational Research Unit,
Cranfield Institute of Technology, Bedford

First published 1979 by
THE MACMILLAN PRESS LTD
London and Basingstoke
Associated companies in Delhi Dublin
Hong Kong Johannesburg Lagos Melbourne
New York Singapore and Tokyo

Typeset by
Reproduction Drawings Ltd, Sutton, Surrey

Printed by

UNWIN BROTHERS LIMITED
The Gresham Press, Old Woking, Surrey

British Library Cataloguing in Publication Data

Murdoch, John, b. *1926* (July)

    Control charts.
    1. Production control—Graphic methods
    I. Title
    658.5'68   TS157

    ISBN 0-333-26411-8
    ISBN 0-333-26412-6 Pbk

Contents

Preface

This book is designed as a practical manual aimed at giving students and management personnel an understanding of the design and use of control charts. The text deals with both the conventional Shewhart type (or British Standard) Charts and the CuSum control charts. Comparisons are included of the operating efficiency of these control schemes at detecting changes. Problems for solution are given at the end of the chapters and fully worked solutions to these problems are included, thus enabling readers to test their understanding at each stage.

The control systems covered in this book are general in their field of application, in that, while usually associated with controlling quality, they can in fact be used to control any management statistic, such as overheads, maintenance, cost, fuel consumption, etc. In this field of management control, the CuSum system shows clearly its superiority over the Shewhart system in that it is equally suitable for a sample size of one which is usually the requirement for general management control systems. The inclusion of Chapter 6, covering the use of the CuSum system as a diagnostic technique is special to this book and a range of practical examples are used to demonstrate the power of the CuSum as a diagnostic management tool, including the now well-known Cranfield Case Study, by my colleague J. A. Barnes, on monitoring a vehicle's fuel consumption. Again, the development of nomograms and tables has simplified the design of both variable and attribute CuSum control systems and Chapter 7 gives full details of the use of these new nomograms and tables.

Since it is usual to link quality control charts to a sampling inspection scheme, an introduction to the principles of the design of sampling inspection schemes is given in the final chapter of the book.

A knowledge of basic statistics including Binomial, Poisson and Normal distributions and significance testing is assumed in readers. However, a revision chapter (Chapter 3) is included, demonstrating the use of statistical theory in control chart design. For readers wishing to revise their basic statistical knowledge, *Statistics: Problems and Solutions*, published by The Macmillan Press, is recommended.

The relevant statistical tables which appear in the appendix at the end of the book are reproduced from Murdoch and Barnes' *Statistical Tables for Science, Engineering, Management and Business Studies* (The Macmillan Press).

Cranfield, 1979   J.M.

Principal Symbols

Roman

A and A'	multipliers of σ and $\bar{w}$ (respectively) to give Shewhart (British) chart limits for process average
A_2	multiplier for Shewhart (American) charts to give limits for process average
b	vertical width of CuSum mask (in CuSum units)
c	acceptance number in single sampling inspection plans
D and D'	*multipliers of σ and $\bar{w}$ (respectively) to give Shewhart (British) chart limits of range*
D_3 and D_4	multipliers for lower and upper limits of range—American-type Charts
d	horizontal width CuSum mask (units = no. of samples)
d_n	range conversion factor, $\sigma = \bar{w}/d_n$
h	decision interval, CuSum control (CuSum units)
I	average amount of inspection/batch
k	reference value CuSum control
L_0	Average Run Length to detection at acceptable quality level (AQL)
L_1	Average Run Length to detection at reject quality level (RQL)
m	average defects/sample
m_1	average defects/sample at acceptable quality level p_1
m_2	average defects/sample at reject quality level p_2
n	sample size
N	batch size
p	batch fraction defective
p_0	process capability (fraction defective) for attribute control
p_1	acceptable quality level (fraction defective)
p_2	reject quality level (fraction defective)
$P(A)$	probability of accepting the batch
$P(R)$	probability of rejecting the batch $= 1 - P(A)$
R	ratio $m_2/m_1 = p_2/p_1$
s	sample standard deviation
S_r	CuSum value after r readings $= \sum_{i=1}^{r}(x_i - k)$
U	standardised normal variate
w	range of a sample
$\bar{w}$	average range

x	variable
$\bar{x}$	sample average
$\bar{X}$	sample average in Shewhart control

Greek

α	risk of rejecting batches of acceptable quality level
β	risk of accepting batches of reject quality level
θ	CuSum mask angle ($^{\circ}$)
σ_0	process capability Shewhart schemes (variable schemes)
σ	process capability CuSum schemes (variable schemes)
μ_0	acceptable quality level (variable schemes)
μ_1	reject quality level (variable schemes)
χ^2	chi-squared value

Author's Note

The use of an asterisk above a table number signifies that the table number is a *Statistical Table* in the Appendix at the end of this book. Thus, table 2* refers to Statistical Table 2 in the appendix—namely, the Normal Distribution.

1. Process Variation

1.1 Introduction

In manufacturing, variations occur in the measured quality of the product, and however controlled the process is, some variation will still occur.

This variation arises from a collection of factors inherent in the process, none of them necessarily large in themselves, but their combined effect is to give variation in the measured quality. In order to fully understand the nature of this variation, we will now briefly consider one of the basic principles of statistics.

1.2 Statistical Concept of Variability

The study of nature's products shows clearly that no two things are exactly alike. Two identical twins are never exactly alike, and one can usually be distinguished from the other. A standard of comparison for similarity is the saying 'alike as two peas'. Yet, study two peas from the same pod, and difference in size or volume or colour or shape will become apparent.

Other things are much more variable. Consider, for example, the heights of men. Heights between 140 cm and 165 cm are quite common and heights outside this range are by no means rare. Reasons for the variation are usually not difficult to find when a particular case is studied. Thus the heights of men are dependent upon a large number of hereditary and environmental causes. When the height of any man picked at random is studied, it will depend upon the chance occurrence of these causes.

Although it is not so obvious, man-made articles are also subject to the same kind of variation. The manufacturer of washers realizes that some washers will have a greater thickness than others. The resistances of electrical filaments made at the same time will not be exactly alike; the running cost of a department in a works will not be exactly the same each week, although there may be no apparent reason for the differences; the tensile strength of a steel bar is not the same at two parts of the same bar; the ash content of coal in a truck is different for samples taken from different positions in the truck; differences will be found in the diameter of components being produced on a lathe and so on.

It is interesting to note that even with the greatest precision of manufacture, variability will still exist providing the measuring equipment is accurate enough to pick it up.

In present-day manufacture, the aim is usually to make things as alike as possible. Or alternatively, the amount of variability permitted is specified so that variation between certain limits is acceptable.

In the case of processes where the quality measure is only assessed as acceptable or not similar arguments apply. The quality measure is the fraction defective and the actual fraction defective found will vary from sample to sample.

Quality measures assessed as fraction defective are called 'attribute' measures and quality measures assessed on the value of characteristics on a continuous scale as 'variable' measures.

1.3   Process Capability

This variation in quality, which is inherent in the process, is known as the *Inherent Process Variation* or the *Process Capability*. Thus the process capability is the measure of the quality standard that the process is capable of meeting under its normal operating conditions. For example, in the case of bar feed automatic lathes, the process capability is given by the quality variation in components made under controlled machine operating conditions, i.e. setting, oil coolants, etc. This process capability is made up of two components:

(a) Variation inherent in the raw material.
(b) Variations inherent in the process itself including operator variations.

However, in practice, other factors which give rise to further variation in measured quality can also occur, i.e. tool wear in automatic lathes, fall of gas pressure in bottle manufacture, choking of tobacco feed systems in cigarette manufacture, variation between operators, etc. These factors are known as *assignable factors*.

Statistical quality control is the name given to techniques for detecting the presence of *assignable factors*, thus enabling diagnosis and correction of the process with a resulting improvement in quality.

The second feature of statistical quality control lies in the fact that, by measuring the process capability and thus specifying that this variation must occur of necessity, many unnecessary adjustments to the process are prevented. These unnecessary adjustments cannot decrease the variation and, in fact must inevitably increase it.

The main use of statistical quality control used to lie in the mass production processes and, to a lesser extent in batch production, but the CuSum control technique (Chapters 6 and 7) now gives a method for applying statistical quality control theory to 'jobbing' or low volume production processes.

1.3.1 The Measure of the Quality of the Product

The Quality of a product can be measured either as:

(a) *Variable* – a measurement on a continuous scale, i.e. volume in litres, length in metres weight in kilograms, hardness in Rockwell units, etc.; or

(b) *Attribute* – Whether or not the product conforms to given specified requirements (e.g. Go/No Go inspection, etc.) and thus the quality is measured as the percentage or the fraction of the products which are defective.

1.4 Measurement of Process Capability

1.4.1 Variable Measures

The first step in a quality control programme is to measure the process capability and to answer the question as to whether or not the process is operating under control.

Production processes are, as stated, never good enough to have no variation. Some processes however have a very high process variation while others are low. Again, even inside the same process, the process capability can vary. For example, in an automatic lathe, the process capability may be less on a diameter dimension than on a length dimension.

Based on statistical theory, if sufficient readings of the quality measure were available under controlled conditions, then the measure of the process variation or quality standard can be assessed, in the case of variables, by measuring the standard deviation of the readings.

$$\text{Process Capability} \quad \sigma_0 = \sqrt{\sum_{i=1}^{n} \frac{(x_i - \bar{x})^2}{n-1}}$$

where x_i = measure of quality on ith unit; $\bar{x}$ = average of the measure of quality of the n units; n = sample size.

In the case of a variable measure, since the sample size n would have to be large in order to give an accurate estimate of the process capability (σ_0) it would be difficult in many cases to guarantee that no assignable factors occurred during the time taken to draw the sample.

It is for this reason that the process capability is estimated by taking a relatively small sample, where it can be safely assumed that process conditions have remained constant, and by repeating these small samples at intervals to give the required accuracy of estimation. In addition, the use of a large number of relatively small samples (sample size $n \leqslant 12$ and preferably $n < 6$) enables use to be made of the average range ($\bar{w}$) of the samples to estimate the process capability, thus greatly simplifying the computation, an important point in the practical application of Control Charts.

1.4.2 Attribute Measure

As with variable measures, a number of samples of size n are taken but in this case, the quality is assessed simply as defective or not. Since the classification of quality is either a defect or not, the use of an attribute measure requires a larger sample size (usually $25 \leqslant n \leqslant 250$) to enable a reliable estimate to be obtained of the process capability of the process.

The process capability of the process is measured as the average fraction defective obtained over the samples or,

The Process Capability $\quad p_0 \;=\; \sum_{i=1}^{m} \dfrac{np_i}{mn}$

where p_i = fraction defective of the ith sample; n = sample size; m = number of samples.

Note It is important that an additional test is carried out to ensure that the process was in control when the samples were drawn (see Chapter 4).

2. Principles of Control

2.1 Introduction

The concepts of statistical control theory as they are used in the design and operation of control charts will now be discussed. It is important to note that these basic principles of control apply to any control problem, e.g. stock control, accidents, overheads, etc., and examples of the use of the control theory to these wider management areas will be given later in the book.

The steps in the statistical approach to management control will now be illustrated with application to a simple process, see figure 2.1, converting raw material into finished goods in one operation.

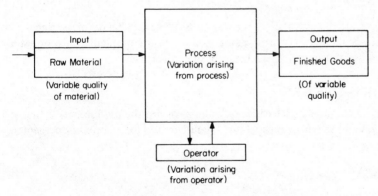

Figure 2.1 A simple process illustrating the sources of variation in finished product

2.2 Setting up Control of a Process

To set up a control system on the process illustrated in figure 2.1 as for any process, the control function set out in figure 2.2 is followed.

The control function is made up of the following steps.

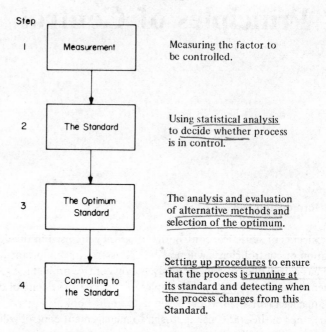

Figure 2.2 The management control function

2.2.1 1st Step -- Measurement

It is not possible to control any process unless one is capable of measuring.
Thus before beginning to control quality some measure of quality must be set up.
As discussed in Chapter 1, the measure of quality is either:

1. An 'Attribute' Measure

The quality measure is on a basis as to whether or not the product meets the
specification and the process capability is measured as the fraction or percentage
defective.
Or
2. A 'Variable' Measure

The quality measure is in terms of some specific characteristic or characteristics of
the component or product measured on a continuous scale, such as:

(i) Measure of quality of canned peas — weight of product in tin in
kilograms; or
(ii) measure of quality of bolt produced — length and diameter of bolt in
centimetres, etc.;

and the process capability is measured by calculating the standard deviation
(σ_0) of the process.

N.B. The distinction between these two types of quality measure must be clearly understood since the control theory used depends on the measure used.

2.2.2 Step 2 – The Standard

This step, namely the setting up of the *standard* for the process is without doubt the most important and it will be seen that *this standard cannot be accurately obtained without the use of statistical theory.*

Consider now any process, and how to define this standard.

What is the standard or process capability? It is not the *best* that the process can do since generally it is always possible to improve by expenditure on resources. In control theory, the standard is defined as the level obtained when the process, operating under its present conditions, is in control or is producing as well as possible. Thus for a process in control or at its standard, the raw material is uniform in quality, the process itself is operating consistently and all operators are equally proficient or in *statistical terms* the probability of any one component being defective is constant over all components.

How then is the standard determined? Here it is necessary to turn to statistical theory.

The *null hypothesis* is set up, namely 'That the process is in control'. Then the distribution of the actual quality measure from current operating conditions is calculated.

If the hypotheses is true, then in the case of attribute measures, the distribution should be *binomial* and in the case of variable measures the distribution should be *normal.*

Thus the hypotheses can be tested by the usual statistical tests. If the process is not in control, then steps must be taken to bring it into control before any further analysis can be carried out. This bringing of the process into control is essentially a management function although statistics can assist.

2.2.3 Step 3 – Deciding the Optimum Standard

Having once decided that the process is at its standard, then the next question is 'Is this the best or optimum operating condition?'. Here many management functions in addition to statistics are involved. The problem involves a comprehensive survey of various methods of improving the process and in some cases an economic consideration of alternative methods of production. Since this book is essentially concerned with the use of statistical methods in bringing processes into control and then holding them in control, the economic analysis involved in this step is not covered.

The important point about this step is that if any change or alteration is made to the process then, before going on to the next step, the fact that the process is in control must again be established. As stated, this step is not included in the control procedures in the book, although clearly it is necessary to fully investigate the alternatives available when applying control theory.

2.2.4 4th Step – Controlling to Standard

This final step in the control function is usually carried out by control charts.

There are two types of control systems – the Shewhart type charts and the CuSum charts. In Britain, there are British Standards for the setting up of Shewhart type charts and the procedures for other countries are similar (see Chapters 4 and 5).

For the CuSum control charts, nomograms and tables have been developed which enable these schemes to be more efficiently designed (see Chapter 7).

3. Statistical Theory in Control Chart Design

3.1 Introduction

This chapter contains a brief revision of the statistical theory used in process control. The techniques covered are the basic concepts of Poisson and normal distributions together with the use of the χ^2 goodness-of-fit test.

Readers who require further study of statistical theory are referred to textbooks on basic statistics[2-4] and for experience in the use of the techniques to the author's book 'Basic Statistics — Problems & Solutions'.[1]

3.2 Review of Basic Statistical Theory in Quality Control

3.2.1 The Binomial Distribution

If the probability of success of an event in a single trial is p and p is constant for all trials, then the probability of x successes in n independent trials is:

$$P(x) = \binom{n}{x} p^x (1-p)^{n-x}$$

3.2.2 The Poisson Distribution

If the chance of an event occurring at any instant is constant in a continuum of time, and if the average number of successes in time t is m, then the probability of x successes in time t is:

$$P(x) = \frac{m^x e^{-m}}{x!}$$

where m = expected (or average) number of successes.

Here, the event's happening had a definite meaning but no meaning can be attached to the event not happening. For example the number of times lightning strikes can be counted and have a meaning but this is not true of the number of times lightning does not strike.

The Poisson Law is important in quality control since this distribution can be used as an approximation to the Binomial distribution whenever the probability of *success p < 0.10* – note in most practical situations the percentage defective is usually well below this level.

Thus, while in process control problems with (attribute measures,) the correct distribution is the (binomial distribution), the simpler (from a computation point of view) Poisson distribution can be used in practice, by setting

the mean $m = np$

Table 1* in Statistical Tables (Appendix) gives the tabulation of the cumulative Poisson probabilities for the mean (m) up to 40. For values of m beyond 40, the normal distribution is used in place of the Poisson distribution.

by setting mean $\mu = np$

and Standard Deviation $\sigma = \sqrt{np\,(1-p)}$

3.2.3 The Normal Distribution

The normal, or Gaussian distribution occupies a central place in the theory of statistics. It is an adequate, and often very good approximation to other distributions which occur.

As stated, when a process is in *control*, where the quality measure is a variable, then readings of this quality measure form a normal distribution.

The equation of the normal distribution is:

$$y = \frac{1}{\sigma\sqrt{2\pi}} \; \exp\left[-\frac{(x - \mu)^2}{2\,\sigma^2} \right]$$

where μ is the mean of the variable x; σ is the standard deviation of x; π is the well-known mathematical constant (= 3.142 approximately).

This equation can be used to derive various properties of the normal distribution. A useful one is the relation between area under the curve and deviation from the mean, but before looking at this we need to refer to a standardised variable.

Any random variable, x, having mean, μ, and standard deviation, σ, can be expressed in standardised form, i.e. x is measured from μ in multiples of σ. The standardised variable is therefore given by $(x-\mu)/\sigma$ and is dimensionless.

In particular, if x is a normal variate then

$$U = \frac{x-\mu}{\sigma}$$

is standardised normal variate.

Area under the Normal Curve

The total area under the normal curve is unity (as is the case for any probability density function) and the area under the curve between two values of x, say a and b (shown shaded in figure 3.1) gives the proportion of the population having

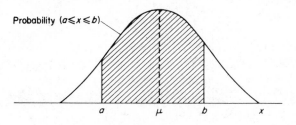

Figure 3.1

values between a and b. This is equal to the probability that a single random value of x will be bigger than a but less than b.

Table 2* in the Appendix gives the area in one tail of the normal distribution, and using the symmetry of the distribution, the table can be used to find the probability of a value between a and b.

3.2.4 Fitting Poisson and Normal Distributions to Data

As will be developed in later chapters, one of the simpler tests for whether or not a process is in *control*, is:

> to fit a *Poisson* distribution to the quality data in the case of an attribute measure, or to fit a *Normal* distribution to the data for a variable measure.

The fitting of distributions to data will now be demonstrated.

Example No. 1 -- Fitting a Poisson Distribution

The number of defects in 57 samples of size $n = 50$ taken from a process are listed in table 3.1.

Table 3.1   No. of defects/sample

1	1	0	2	3	3	5	2	2	1	4	4
2	3	3	3	2	2	1	0	4	6	2	5
6	1	4	1	4	3	4	2	7	6	1	2
3	6	4	2	1	4	3	3	3	6	8	3
5	3	3	2	1	3	5	3	5			

Fit a Poisson distribution to this data.

Data is first summarised into a distribution (table 3.2).

Table 3.2

No. of defects	0	1	2	3	4	5	6	7	8	Total
Frequency	2	9	11	15	8	5	5	1	1	57

Table 3.3

No. of defects/sample	0	1	2	3	4	5	6	7	8	Total
Poisson probability[1] distribution	0.045	0.140	0.217	0.223	0.173	0.107	0.056	0.024	0.0142	1.000
Poisson frequency[2] distribution	2.6	7.98	12.4	12.7	9.9	6.1	3.2	1.4	0.8	57
Actual frequency distribution	2	9	11	15	8	5	5	1	1	57

[1] The Poisson probabilities are obtained from Table 1*.
[2] The Poisson frequency is the Poisson probability × No. of readings.

Calculation of the mean,

Average defects/sample $(m) = \dfrac{(2 \times 0) + (9 \times 1) + \ldots (1 \times 7) + (1 \times 8)}{57}$

$= 3.1$

With the average defects/sample $= 3.1$, a Poisson distribution with the same mean $(m = 3.1)$ is fitted to the data (table 3.3 opposite).

3.2.5 Example No.2 – Fitting a Normal Distribution to Data

The production time/unit of a process is given in table 3.4 for 60 units. Fit a Normal Distribution to the data.

Table 3.4   Production time. Basic minutes per cycle

0.09	0.09	0.11	0.09	0.09	0.11	0.09	0.07	0.09	0.06
0.09	0.09	0.09	0.11	0.09	0.07	0.09	0.06	0.10	0.07
0.09	0.10	0.06	0.10	0.08	0.06	0.09	0.08	0.08	0.08
0.08	0.10	0.08	0.07	0.09	0.08	0.09	0.11	0.09	0.09
0.08	0.10	0.09	0.08	0.10	0.08	0.08	0.09	0.09	0.09
0.08	0.06	0.08	0.08	0.10	0.09	0.09	0.10	0.10	0.11

First summarise the data into a distribution. Range $= 0.11 - 0.06 = 0.05$. The data is shown summarised into a distribution in table 3.5.

Table 3.5   Production time

Class interval	Mid-pt (x_i)	Frequency (f_i)
0.055 – 0.065	0.06	5
0.065 – 0.075	0.07	4
0.075 – 0.085	0.08	14
0.085 – 0.095	0.09	23
0.095 – 0.105	0.10	9
0.105 – 0.115	0.11	5
Total	Σf_i	60

Calculation of Mean and Standard Deviation

The calculation of the mean and standard deviation is shown below using the transform

$$u_i = \frac{x_i - x_0}{c}$$

where x_0 = given value of variable; c = class interval width.
   Here let $x_0 = 0.09$ min; $c = 0.01$ min.
   The computations are shown in table 3.6.

Table 3.6

Class interval	Mid. pt. (x_i)	Frequency (f_i)	u_i	$u_i f_i$	$u_i^2 f_i$
0.055 – 0.065	0.06	5	−3	−15	45
0.065 – 0.075	0.07	4	−2	−8	16
0.075 – 0.085	0.08	14	−1	−14	14
0.085 – 0.095	0.09	23	0	0	0
0.095 – 0.105	0.10	9	+1	+9	9
0.105 – 0.115	0.11	5	+2	+10	20
				$\Sigma u_i f_i = -18$	$\Sigma u_i^2 f_i = 104$

Table 3.7

Class	Class boundary	Standardised upper boundary 'u'	Upper tail area of N.D. above 'u'	Area in each class	Expected normal frequency	Observed class frequency
1	2	3	4	5	6	7
0.035–0.045	0.045	−3.23	1−0.0007 = 0.9993	0.0007	–	0
0.045–0.055	0.055	−2.46	1−0.0070 = 0.9930	0.0063	0.4	0
0.055–0.065	0.065	−1.69	1−0.0455 = 0.9545	0.0385	2.3	5
0.065–0.075	0.075	−0.92	1−0.1788 = 0.8212	0.1333	8.0	4
0.075–0.085	0.085	−0.15	1−0.4404 = 0.5596	0.2616	15.7	14
0.085–0.095	0.095	0.62	0.2676	0.2920	17.5	23
0.095–0.105	0.105	1.38	0.0838	0.1838	11.0	9
0.105–0.115	0.115	2.15	0.0158	0.0680	4.1	5
0.115–0.125	0.125	2.92	0.0018	0.0140	0.8	0
				0.9982	59.8	60

The mean $\bar{x} = x_0 + \dfrac{\Sigma u_i f_i}{\Sigma f_i}$ and standard deviation

$$s = c\sqrt{\dfrac{\Sigma u_i^2 f - \dfrac{(\Sigma u_i f_i)^2}{\Sigma f_i}}{\Sigma f_i - 1}}$$

from table 3.6.

$\Sigma u_i f_i = -18 \quad \Sigma f_i = 104$

$\Sigma u_i^2 f_i = 104$

Hence the mean $\bar{x} = x_0 + c\,\dfrac{\Sigma u_i f_i}{\Sigma f i}$

$= 0.09 + 0.01 \times \dfrac{(-18)}{60}$

$= 0.087$ min

The standard deviation

$$s = c\sqrt{\dfrac{\Sigma u_i^2 f_i - \dfrac{(\Sigma u_i f_i)^2}{\Sigma f_i}}{\Sigma f_i - 1}}$$

$= 0.01\sqrt{\dfrac{104 - \dfrac{(-18)^2}{60}}{(60-1)}}$

Therefore
$s = 0.013$ min

Fitting a Normal Distribution to the Data

Here the mean $\bar{x} = 0.087$ min, and the standard deviation $s = 0.013$ min.

The fitting of a normal distribution to this data is summarised in table 3.7.

Table 2* is used to give the area in the tail of the normal distribution. Thus, the area below 0.045 is obtained as follows:

$$u_i = \dfrac{x_i - \bar{x}}{s} = \dfrac{0.045 - 0.087}{0.013} = -3.23 \approx -3.2$$

From table 2*, area below 0.045 = 0.0007. Thus area above 0.045 = 1−0.0007 = 0.9993, 4th column of table 3.6. Probabilities to four decimal places.

Again area above 0.055 = 1-0.0070 = 0.9930. Thus normal probability for the class interval 0.045 – 0.055 = 0.9993-0.9930 = 0.0063 etc., 5th column of table 3.6.

Finally the expected normal frequency is obtained by multiplying these normal probabilities by the total number of readings.

3.2.6 χ^2 *Goodness-of-Fit Test*

An important use of the χ^2 distribution is as a significance test for 'goodness-of-fit' between observed data and a hypothesis.

Let k = number of cells or comparisons; O_i = observed frequency in ith cell; E_i = expected frequency in ith cell from the hypothesis; r = number of restrictions, derived from the observed readings, which have to be used when fitting the hypothesis.

Then the sum
$$\chi^2 = \sum_{i=1}^{k} \frac{(O_i - E_i)^2}{E_i}$$

is distributed like χ^2 with $(k-r)$ degrees of freedom.

When fitting distributions, the constraints are:

(1) Making total frequency of the distributions the same – one constraint.
(2) Number of parameters used to fit the distributions — these parameters being calculated from the data.

Thus, when fitting a normal distribution — the number of constraints is 3, or:

1 for the total frequency;
1 for using the mean in fitting the normal distribution;
1 for using the standard deviation in fitting the normal distribution.

Again when fitting a Poisson distribution the number of constraints is only 2, or:

1 for the total frequency;
1 for using the mean in fitting the Poisson distribution
(the standard deviation is not required).

N.B. In this test, all the E_i values must be greater than 5. If any are less, then the data must be grouped.
Table 3* in the Appendix gives values of the χ^2 function.

Examples
No.1: Testing the Significance of the Fit of a Poisson Distribution to Data

Use Example No. 1 on page 11. In this example, it is necessary to group the first two classes and the last three classes in order to meet the requirement that all expected class frequencies are higher than 5, see table 3.8.

Table 3.8

No. of defects/samples	0	1	2	3	4	5	6	7	8	Total
Actual frequency (O)	2	9	11	15	8	5	5	1	1	57
	$\underbrace{\quad}_{11}$						$\underbrace{\qquad}_{7}$			
Poisson frequency (E)	2.6	8.0	12.4	12.7	9.9	6.1	3.2	1.4	0.8	57
	$\underbrace{\quad}_{10.6}$						$\underbrace{\qquad}_{5.4}$			

$$\therefore \chi^2 = \frac{(11-10.6)^2}{10.6} + \frac{(11-12.4)^2}{12.4} + \ldots + \frac{(5-6.1)^2}{6.1} +. \frac{(7-5.4)^2}{5.4} = 1.63$$

Degrees of freedom = 6−1−1 = 4, since the totals are made the same and the Poisson distribution is fitted with same mean as the actual distribution.

Referring to Table 3*.

$$\chi^2_{0.05} = 9.488; \qquad \chi^2_{0.01} = 13.277$$

Thus, since the χ^2 value of 1.63 is well below the significance levels, there is no evidence of the process being out of *control*.

No. 2: Testing the Significance of the Fit of a Normal Distribution to Data

The data from Example No. 2, page 13 will be used. Table 3.9 gives the actual frequency distribution together with the normal frequency distribution fitted to the data — see pages 14 and 15.

Table 3.9

Class interval (i)	Actual frequency (O_i)	Normal frequency (E_i)	Contribution to χ^2_i
0.045 – 0.055	0 ⎫	0.4 ⎫	
0.055 – 0.065	5 ⎬ 9	2.3 ⎬ 10.7	0.27
0.065 – 0.075	4 ⎭	8.0 ⎭	
0.075 – 0.085	14	15.7	0.18
0.085 – 0.095	23	17.5	1.72
0.095 – 0.105	9 ⎫	11.0 ⎫	
0.105 – 0.115	5 ⎬ 14	4.1 ⎬ 15.9	0.23
0.115 – 0.125	0 ⎭	0.8 ⎭	
			$\chi^2 = 2.40$

Again the first three classes and the last three classes have had to be grouped to give $E_i > 5$. The χ^2 values are given in the last column.

Degrees of freedom = 4 − 2 − 1 = 1, from Table 3*.

Significance levels

$$\chi^2_{0.05} = 3.841$$

$$\chi^2_{0.01} = 6.635$$

$$\chi^2_{0.001} = 10.827$$

Here χ^2 is not significant, and thus there is no evidence that process is *out of control*.

References

1. J. Murdoch and J. A. Barnes (1973). *Statistics: Problems and Solutions.* The Macmillan Press Ltd., New York
2. J. F. Ratcliffe (1967). *Elements of Mathematical Statistics.* Oxford University Press
3. Richard Goodman (1970). *Teach Yourself Statistics.* The English Universities Press Ltd., London
4. M. J. Moroney (1952). *Facts From Figures.* Penguin Books Ltd., Harmondsworth

4. Process Capability

4.1 Introduction

The measurement of process capability is carried out by taking a number of relatively small samples from the process at regular intervals of time and analysing the data to ensure that no assignable factors are present. In practice a minimum of 25 samples are required and the sample size taken depends on many factors, including production rate of process, cost of measurement, etc.

The range of sample sizes and the most commonly employed sizes are given in table 4.1 for both attribute and variable schemes.

Table 4.1   Sample sizes for process capability studies

	Range of sample sizes	Most commonly used sample sizes
Attribute measure	$25 \leqslant n \leqslant 250$	50, 100 and 200
Variable measure	$2 \leqslant n \leqslant 12$	4 and 5

The period over which the samples are drawn should cover sufficient output and time to enable the presence of assignable factors to be detected if they are present.

4.2   Measurement of Process Capability

4.2.1   Variable Measures

In the case of variable measures, consider the following m samples of size n (table 4.2).

The samples are drawn from the process at regular intervals e.g. every hour,

Table 4.2

			Sample No.		
1	2	. . . .	i	. . . .	m
x_{11}	x_{21}	. . . .	x_{i1}	. . . .	x_{m1}
x_{12}	x_{22}	. . . .	x_{i2}	. . . .	x_{m2}
x_{13}	x_{23}	. . . .	x_{i3}	. . . .	x_{m3}
.	.	. . . .	.	. . . .	.
x_{1n}	x_{2n}	. . . .	x_{in}	. . . .	x_{mn}
Sample means $\bar{X}_1$	$\bar{X}_2$	. . . .	$\bar{X}_i$	. . . .	X_m
Sample range w_1	w_2	. . . .	w_i	. . . .	w_m

every 10 min, etc. dependent on the process, and since the sample size is small ($n < 12$) it can be stated that within a sample no assignable causes are present.

Thus the process capability can be measured by pooling all the individual sample estimates of the standard deviation of the process.

$$\text{Process capability } \sigma_0 = \sqrt{\sum_{i=1}^{m} \sum_{j=1}^{n} \frac{(x_{ij} - \bar{x}_i)^2}{m(n-1)}}$$

However this calculation is long and laborious and in practice use is made of Hartleys' conversion constant (d_n) for estimating the process capability or standard deviation from the average range ($\bar{w}$) of the samples. The individual range of each sample, w_i is calculated and the average range size ($\bar{w}$) obtained from the n individual sample ranges.

Then

Process capability $\sigma_0 = \bar{w}/d_n$ where $\bar{w}$ = average range; d_n = Hartley's conversion constant.

The values of d_n for sample size n from 2 to 12 are given in table 4.3 – the values of d_n are also listed in the last column of table 6* of the statistical tables at the end of the book.

4.2.2 Attribute Measures

Again with attribute measures a number of samples of size n are drawn. Since, however, only a classification into defective or not is involved, the sample size n has to be larger (usually between 25 and 250) depending on the process.

The process capability $p_0 = \dfrac{\textit{Total defects in all samples}}{mn}$

where m = number of samples; n = sample size.

Here, since it is not possible to eliminate between sample variation from the

Table 4.3   Hartley's conversion constant (d_n)

Sample size (n)	Conversion constant (d_n)
2	1.128
3	1.693
4	2.059
5	2.326
6	2.534
7	2.704
8	2.847
9	2.970
10	3.078
11	3.173
12	3.258

estimate of process capability a check is required on whether or not the process has been in control over the period that the samples were drawn. If the process is in control, then the number of defects/sample should conform to a Poisson distribution. Thus checking whether the sample data agrees with a Poisson distribution gives a check on whether or not the process was in control. If the process is not in control, then the estimate of process capability is not correct and the process should be brought into control before further samples are drawn and the process capability reassessed.

In the case of variable measures, no such check is required, since the estimate of process capability is independent of any between sample variation.

4.3   Examples on the Estimation of Process Capability

No.1:   Bottle Manufacture

The diameter of the welt measurements on 25 samples of size 4 taken every 20 minutes from an automatic bottle production process are given in table 4.4. Calculate the process capability on welt diameter and discuss the tolerance which the process can achieve.

Solution

The Average Range $\bar{w} = \dfrac{0.2 + 0.2 + 0.4 + \ldots + 0.3 + 0.2 + 0.1}{25}$

$$= 0.204$$

From table 4.2 (or table 6*) for $n = 4$ Hartley's conversion constant $d_n = 2.059$.

Therefore process capability $\sigma_0 = \dfrac{0.204}{2.059} \doteq 0.10 \text{ mm}$

Table 4.4 Welt diameter (mm)

Sample No.	1	2	3	4	5	6	7	8	9
	13.9	14.0	13.8	14.1	14.2	14.0	14.1	14.1	14.0
	14.0	14.0	14.2	14.1	14.0	14.1	14.3	13.9	14.1
	14.0	13.9	14.0	13.8	14.0	14.0	14.1	14.1	13.9
	14.1	13.8	14.2	14.1	14.0	14.0	13.9	14.1	14.1
Sample mean $\overline{X}$	14.00	13.90	14.05	14.03	14.05	14.00	14.10	14.05	14.03
Sample range w	0.2	0.2	0.4	0.3	0.2	0.1	0.4	0.2	0.2

Sample No.	10	11	12	13	14	15	16	17	18
	14.0	14.1	14.1	14.2	14.1	14.0	13.9	14.0	13.9
	14.1	13.9	14.0	13.8	14.0	13.9	14.0	13.8	14.1
	14.0	13.9	14.0	14.1	14.0	14.1	13.9	13.9	14.0
	14.1	14.0	13.9	13.8	14.0	14.0	13.9	13.9	14.1
Sample mean $\overline{X}$	14.05	13.98	14.00	13.98	14.03	14.00	13.93	13.90	14.03
Sample range w	0.1	0.2	0.2	0.4	0.1	0.2	0.1	0.2	0.2

Sample No.	19	20	21	22	23	24	25		
	13.9	14.0	13.9	14.1	13.8	13.9	14.0		sample means
	13.9	14.0	14.1	13.9	14.1	14.1	14.1		correct to two
	14.0	14.1	14.1	14.1	14.0	14.0	14.1		decimal places
	14.0	14.1	13.8	13.9	14.1	14.0	14.0		
Sample mean $\overline{X}$	13.90	14.05	13.98	14.00	14.00	14.00	14.05		
Sample range w	0.1	0.1	0.3	0.1	0.3	0.2	0.1		

Thus this process can produce bottles to a welt diameter $\pm 1.96\sigma_0$ or $\pm$ 0.20 mm (approximately) with 95% confidence or to a welt diameter $\pm 2.58\sigma_0$ or ± 0.26 mm with 99% confidence.

However this tolerance can only be achieved if the process is always producing to a process average which is at the centre of the tolerance range. In practice, processes require some play or movement of process average and based on samples taken, an estimate ± 0.10 mm for this play would appear adequate.

Thus the tolerance which process can meet with 95% confidence is ± 0.30 mm.

No.2: Production Process

Samples of size $n = 200$ taken every four hours from an automatic process gave the number of defects/sample over 50 samples shown in table 4.5. Calculate the process capability.

Table 4.5   Number of defects/sample

	1 – 10	2	6	4	5	1	3	2	1	4	2
	11 – 20	0	4	6	3	4	3	2	4	5	4
Sample No.	21 – 30	3	6	3	0	7	4	7	3	5	4
	31 – 40	3	2	0	5	2	5	3	2	9	3
	41 – 50	0	1	1	0	3	5	1	4	1	5

Solution

The first step is to summarise this data into a distribution and to calculate the average defects/sample. Table 4.6. gives the distribution.

Table 4.6

	No. of defects/sample										
No. of Defects	0	1	2	3	4	5	6	7	8	9	Total
Frequency	5	6	7	10	9	7	3	2	0	1	50

$$\text{Average defects/sample} = \frac{5 \times 0 + 6 \times 1 + \ldots\ldots\ldots + 0 \times 8 + 1 \times 9}{50}$$

$$= 3.2 \text{ defects/sample of } 200$$

or an estimated process defective rate of 1.6%.

This defective rate of 1.6% will be the estimate of the process capability only if the process has been *in control* over the period over which the samples were drawn.

This assumption can be checked by comparing the actual distribution of defects/sample with the theoretical Poisson distribution which would occur if process was in control.

Table 4.7

No. of defects/sample	0	1	2	3	4	5	6	7	8	9	Total
Actual frequency	5	6	7	10	9	7	3	2	0	1	50
	⎰ 11 ⎱						⎰ 6 ⎱				
[a]Poisson probability	0.04	0.13	0.21	0.22	0.18	0.11	0.06	0.03	0.01	0.01	1.000
Poisson frequency	2.0	6.5	10.5	11.5	9.0	5.5	3.0	1.5	0.5	0.5	50.0
	⎰ 8.5 ⎱						⎰ 5.5 ⎱				

[a]From Table 1* (rounded off to two decimal places).

This answer is obtained by setting up a hypothesis stating 'That the process is in control' and testing this hypothesis (called a *null hypothesis*).

If the process is in control over the period covered by the samples, then the chance of any one component being defective has been constant for every component — this must be true for the process to be in control — and therefore the distribution of the number of defects will be *Binomial* and in cases when the process capability is less than 10%, then the *Poisson distribution* can be used as an approximation to the *Binomial distribution*.

N.B. Most textbooks and tables assume that quality control theory is only applied to processes with process capabilities below 10%, and therefore use this Poisson approximation.

Table 4.7 gives the comparison of the actual distribution and the theoretical Poisson distribution.

Comparing the Poisson frequency distribution and the actual frequency distribution shows generally good agreement and this agreement is confirmed by a χ^2 test.

$$\chi^2 = \frac{(11-9.5)^2}{9.5} + \frac{(7-10.5)^2}{10.5} + \frac{(10-11.5)^2}{11.5} + \frac{(9-9)^2}{9} + \frac{(7-5.5)^2}{5.5} + \frac{(6-5.5)^2}{5.5}$$

$$= 0.24 + 1.17 + 0.20 + 0 + 0.41 + 0.045 = 2.07$$

Degrees of freedom $(\nu) = 6 - 1 - 1 = 4$. Referring to Table 3*, it will be seen that χ^2 with 4 degrees of freedom has to exceed 9.488 for significance at 5% level. Therefore the χ^2 test shows no evidence that the process is not in control.

Thus the estimate of process capability is 1.6% defective.

No.3: Machine Breakdowns

To demonstrate further the application of control theory, table 4.8 gives the number of machine breakdowns/per week over the last 50 weeks in a large automatic machine shop with 200 similar type machines. Does this data signify that the maintenance policy is 'in control'?

Table 4.8 No. of breakdowns/week

Week No.										
1 – 10	0	4	3	6	2	0	1	1	0	1
11 – 20	1	3	0	0	3	0	5	0	0	1
21 – 30	0	1	4	2	0	1	5	0	5	6
31 – 40	4	1	5	0	2	4	4	1	1	0
41 – 50	5	2	0	1	1	5	0	4	0	5

Solution

Clearly the control theory developed for quality control can be applied to control any variable. In the case of attributes, examples include accidents, breakdowns, number of stock-outs, etc.

A hypothesis is set up, namely — that the maintenance policy over the 50 wk period has been 'in control' or there have been no assignable factors present, i.e. the probability of a breakdown has been constant over the 50 wk period and this probability is the same for all machines.

Thus the breakdown data should conform to a Poisson distribution if hypothesis is true.

Table 4.9 gives this data summarised into a frequency distribution together with the Poisson distribution fitted to this data.

Table 4.9

No. of breakdowns/wk	0	1	2	3	4	5	6	Total
Frequency	16	12	4	3	6	7	2	50
						15		
Poisson probability[a]	0.14	0.27	0.27	0.18	0.09	0.04	0.02	1.01
Poisson frequency	7	13.5	13.5	9	4.5	2	1.0	50.5
						7.5		

[a] From table 1*.

$$\text{Average defects/sample } m = \frac{16 \times 0 + 1 \times 12 + \ldots\ldots + 7 \times 5 + 2 \times 6}{50}$$

$$= 2.0$$

The χ^2 test gives:

$$\chi^2 = \frac{(16-7)^2}{7} + \frac{(12-13.5)^2}{13.5} + \frac{(4-13.5)^2}{13.5} + \frac{(3-9)^2}{9} + \frac{(15-7.5)^2}{7.5}$$

$$= 11.6 + 0.17 + 6.7 + 4 + 7.5$$

$$= 29.97$$

For 3 df this result is highly significant (see table 3*), confirming the apparent disagreement and that the system is *not in control*.

This example will be further discussed in Chapter 6 to demonstrate the use of CuSum charts in diagnosing when changes in the Breakdown Rate have occurred.

No.4: *Food Production Process*

In the production of cans of soup, the nominal weight is 0.5 kg. Thirty samples of six cans taken from the process gave an average range ($\bar{w}$) of 0.02 kg.

Table 4.10

Sample No.	1	2	3	4	5	6	7	8	9	10	11	12
	6.23	6.29	6.19	6.24	6.20	6.31	6.19	6.25	6.27	6.25	6.20	6.28
	6.23	6.21	6.25	6.20	6.20	6.29	6.27	6.14	6.23	6.20	6.22	6.22
	6.20	6.17	6.18	6.19	6.21	6.19	6.16	6.23	6.25	6.21	6.12	6.24
Size (mm)	6.26	6.27	6.27	6.23	6.32	6.23	6.21	6.24	6.22	6.29	6.25	6.23
	6.29	6.27	6.20	6.19	6.17	6.19	6.14	6.25	6.27	6.18	6.23	6.13
	6.27	6.14	6.25	6.28	6.21	6.33	6.26	6.17	6.26	6.15	6.12	6.19
	6.28	6.24	6.22	6.08	6.13	6.26	6.30	6.16	6.28	6.29	6.17	6.27
	6.11	6.29	6.19	6.34	6.19	6.27	6.19	6.22	6.17	6.21	6.23	6.25
Mean $\bar{X}$	6.23	6.24	6.22	6.22	6.20	6.26	6.22	6.21	6.24	6.23	6.19	6.23
Range w	0.18	0.15	0.09	0.26	0.19	0.14	0.16	0.11	0.11	0.14	0.13	0.15

What is the process capability and comment on tolerance which process is capable of meeting?

Solution

Here average range $\bar{w} = 0.02$ kg. Hence process capability $\sigma_0 = 0.02/d_n$ for $n = 6$ (from table 6*, $d_n = 2.534$)

$$\sigma_0 = \frac{0.02}{2.534} = 0.008 \text{ kg}$$

Thus with a given process average $(\bar{x})$ the process can produce to $\bar{x} \pm$ 1.96 × 0.008 kg with 95% confidence. However in practice some 'float' or movement in process average would inevitably occur during production, and the tolerance is therefore ± 0.016 kg plus some allowance for the estimated float in the process average.

4.4   Problems for solution

Note: In order to reduce the computation time, the number of samples given has been reduced in the following problems. In practice a minimum of 25 samples would be required.

No. 1

The results of 12 samples of size 8 of the outside diameter measurement of glass tubes used in bottle production are given in table 4.10. The samples are taken every 40 min from the process. Calculate the process capability.

No. 2

Samples of $n = 100$ taken every hour from a process gave the number of defects per sample shown in table 4.11. Calculate the process capability.

Table 4.11

0	1	2	0	3 .	4 .	1	4 .	2	3 .
1	0	1	2	3.	1	4	3,	0	1
2	1	4.	1	1	1	2	3·	1	5
0	0	2	5	2	7	2	0	1	2
2	2	1	3,	5	6	1	1	2	3 .

No. 3

The process average of production unit is 20.00 mm, and the process capability is 1.00 mm. If the tolerance is 20.00 mm ± 2.2 mm, what is the minimum percentage defective which the process will produce? If the process average changes to 20.15 mm, what will the percentage outside tolerance now be?

No. 4

The results of 10 samples of size $n = 5$ from a production process are given in table 4.12. Calculate the process capability.

Table 4.12   Readings coded (measurement in mm − 50) × 100

Sample No.	1	2	3	4	5	6	7	8	9	10
	11	14	20	19	19	14	21	12	14	21
	18	21	21	18	20	13	16	13	14	13
	14	19	21	26	16	16	21	19	22	16
	14	16	24	14	9	17	17	15	14	22
	18	18	20	16	16	16	21	14	22	22

No. 5

The number of defects per shift from a large indexing machine are given in table 4.13 for the last 52 shifts. The production per shift is approximately 600 units. What is the process capability?

Table 4.13

2	6	4	5	1	8	2	1	4	2	7
3	4	3	2	4	5	4	3	6	3	0
7	3	5	8	3	2	6	5	2	5	
5	3	2	1	1	0	3	3	1	4	
3	1	4	7	2	3	6	4	9	2	

4.5   Solutions to problems

No.1

Average range $\bar{w} = \dfrac{0.18 + 0.15 + \ldots + 0.13 + 0.15}{12}$

$= 0.151$ mm

From table 4.2, for $n = 8$ $d_n = 2.847$

Therefore process capability $\sigma = \dfrac{0.151}{2.847}$

$= 0.053$ mm

Thus this process can produce to $\pm 1.96 \times 0.053$ mm or ± 0.106 mm although in practice some additional allowance may be necessary for 'float' in process average.

No.2

The data is summarised in a distribution given in table 4.14.

Table 4.14

No. of defects/sample	0	1	2	3	4	5	6	7	Total
Frequency	7	15	12	7	4	3	1	1	50

$$\text{Average defects/sample} = \frac{7 \times 0 + 15 \times 1 + \ldots + 3 \times 5 + 1 \times 6 + 1 \times 7}{50}$$

$$= 2.08$$

$$= 2.08 \approx 2.1$$

A 'null hypothesis' is set up, namely that process is in control. The Poisson distribution fitted to the data is given in table 4.15 together with the χ^2 test of significance.

Table 4.15

No. of defects	0	1	2	3	4	5	6	7	Total
Frequency	7	15	12	7	4	3	1	1	50
						9			
Poisson probability[a]	0.12	0.26	0.27	0.19	0.10	0.04	0.015	0.006	0.991
Poisson frequency	6	13	13.5	9.5	5.0	2.0	0.75	0.30	50.05
							8.05		

[a] From table 1* (rounded off to 2 significant figures).

$$\text{Therefore } \chi^2 = \frac{(7-6)^2}{6} + \frac{(15-13)^2}{13} + \frac{(12-13.5)^2}{13.5} + \frac{(7-9.5)^2}{9.5} + \frac{(9-8.05)^2}{8.05}$$

$$= 0.17 + 0.31 + 0.17 + 0.67 + 0.12$$

$$= 1.44 \text{ with df } = 5-1-1 = 3$$

Check it out!!

From Table 3* $\chi^2_{0.05} = 7.815$

7.815

Thus χ^2 is clearly *not significant*, therefore there is no evidence that the process is out of control. Thus the process capability is 0.021 fraction defective or 2.1% defective.

No. 3

Assume normal distribution (figure 4.1).

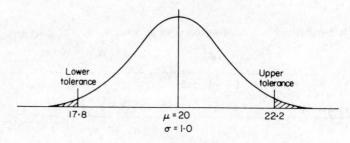

Figure 4.1

$$U = \frac{22.2 - 20}{1.0} = 2.2 \text{ (from table 2*)}$$

Area outside upper tolerance = 0.0139

Therefore fraction outside tolerance = 2×0.0139

$$= 0.0276 \text{ or } 2.76\%$$

If process average changes to 20.15 (figure 4.2),

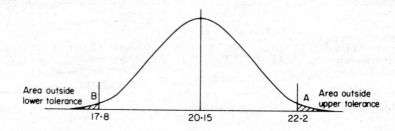

Figure 4.2

For B, $U = \dfrac{17.8 - 20.15}{1.0} = 2.35$ Area = 0.00939 (from table 2*)

For A, $U = \dfrac{22.2 - 20.15}{1.0} = 2.05$ Area = 0.02018

Therefore total outside tolerance (A+ B) = 0.02957 or approximately 3%.

No. 4 Table 4.16 gives the sample average over ranges.

Average range $\bar{w} = \dfrac{7 + 7 + \ldots + 8 + 9}{10} = 7.4$

for $n = 5$ $d_n = 2.326$ (from table 6*)

Table 4.16

Sample No.	1	2	3	4	5	6	7	8	9	10
	11	14	20	19	19	14	21	12	14	21
	18	21	21	18	20	13	16	13	14	13
	14	19	21	26	16	16	21	19	22	16
	14	16	24	14	9	17	17	15	14	22
	18	18	20	16	16	16	21	14	22	22
Range w	7	7	4	12	11	4	5	7	8	9
Average $\bar{X}$	15	17.6	21.2	18.6	16	15.2	19.2	14.6	17.2	18.8

Therefore process capability $\sigma_0 = \dfrac{7.4}{2.326} = 3.18 \approx 3.2$

$$= 0.032 \text{ mm (in original units)}$$

No. 5

The number of defects/shifts data is summarised in a distribution given in table 4.17.

Table 4.17

No. of Defects	0	1	2	3	4	5	6	7	8	9	Total
Frequency	2	6	9	11	8	6	4	3	2	1	52

Average defects/shift $= \dfrac{2 \times 0 + 6 \times 1 + 9 \times 2 + \ldots + 2 \times 8 + 1 \times 9}{52}$

$$= 3.6$$

Hypothesis that process is in *control* is tested by fitting a Poisson distribution with mean $m = 3.6$ to the data.

Poisson distribution is shown fitted in table 4.18 together with χ^2 test.

To test hypothesis that process is in control,

$\chi^2 = \dfrac{(8-6.8)^2}{6.8} + \dfrac{(9-8.8)^2}{8.8} + \dfrac{(11-11)^2}{11} + \dfrac{(8-9.9)^2}{9.9} + \dfrac{(6-7.3)^2}{7.3} + \dfrac{(10-7.8)^2}{7.8}$

$$= 1.43$$

Table 4.18

No. of defects	0	1	2	3	4	5	6	7	8	9	Total
Frequency	2	6	9	11	8	6	4	3	2	1	52
Poisson probability	0.03	0.10	0.17	0.21	0.19	0.14	0.08	0.04	0.02	0.01	1.00
Poisson frequency	1.6	5.2	8.8	11.0	9.9	7.3	4.2	2.1	1.0	0.05	5.16

Frequency: 0 and 1 grouped → 8; 6, 7, 8, 9 grouped → 10.0

Poisson frequency: 0 and 1 grouped → 6.8; 6, 7, 8, 9 grouped → 7.8

Reference to table 3* gives for 4 df $\chi^2_{0.05} = 9.488$

$$\chi^2_{0.01} = 13.377$$

Thus the χ^2 value is not significant. The process capability $= \dfrac{3.6}{600} \times 100\% = 0.6\%$.

5. Shewhart Control Charts

5.1 Introduction

The concept of a control chart was evolved by Dr. Shewhart in America in 1924 – the initial development in Britain being mainly by Dr. Dudding and W. Jennett. Dr. Shewhart suggested that the control chart should have three main objectives.

(1) To define the goal or 'standard' for a process which management should strive to attain.
(2) To be used as an aid to the attaining of this standard.
(3) To serve as a basis for judging whether the standard has been achieved.

Thus the control chart concepts of Shewhart cover the fields of product specification, production and inspection, and when used, assist in integrating these phases of industry.

5.2 Basic Concepts of Shewhart Control Charts

If in a process, the only sources of variation are chance variations, then these chance variations plotted against time will behave in a random manner. In actual fact, as discussed in earlier chapters, in the case of attribute measures, these chance variations will form a *Binomial distribution* and in the case of variable measures, a *Normal distribution*

With attribute measures, providing the probability of a defect (p) is less than 0.10, then the *Poisson distribution* can be used as an approximation to the *Binomial* – thus greatly simplifying the computation.

The knowledge of this behaviour of chance variations of processes when in control is the basis of control chart theory – thus, if the data do not behave in this random manner, then assignable factors are present.

The Shewhart control chart consists of a plot against time of the sample values – the sample average ($\bar{X}$) and sample range (w) in the case of variable measures and the number of defects in the sample for attribute measures – and the setting of limits on these charts to indicate when the process has gone out of control.

36

The limits on the control chart are probability limits and they are determined such that, if only chance causes are present or the process is in *control*, then the probability of a sample point falling outside is very small.

The probability values assigned to the limits are arbitrary and although differences exist between the American and British chart practice, the differences are minor in the case of variable chart design but as will be shown later, there are larger differences in the practice for attribute charts.

The British use two limits, the *warning* and *action* limits, which are essentially probability limits set at 0.025 and 0.001 respectively. In the *USA*, only outer *action* limits are used, set at ± 3 standard deviations from the average.

Consider the British limits:

(1) *The warning limits* — where there is only a 1 in 40 chance (0.025) of a sample point falling outside either limit if the process is in control.

(2) *The action limits* — where there is only a 1 in 1000 chance (0.001) of a sample point falling outside either limit if the process is in control.

In the case of attribute measures, these limits are obtained directly from the Poisson distribution table in table 1*.

For variable measures, the normal distribution tabulated in table 2* is used. Thus from table 2*

warning limits   Process average $\pm 1.96 \; \sigma/\sqrt{n}$

action limits   Process average $\pm 3.09 \; \sigma/\sqrt{n}$

Now, for the American limits, no inner or warning limits are used, and since the probability values chosen for the limits are arbitrary, the American practice is to set the outer limit as process average ± 3 standard deviations for both variable and attribute measures. Thus in the case of attributes, an assumption that the normal distribution can be used as an approximation to the binomial is made.

Thus the limits for attributes are:

$$np \pm 3\sqrt{np_0 \, (1-p_0)}$$

The American practice is thus designed for simplicity in application by having limits set always at ± 3 standard deviations.

Both types of chart will be illustrated in this chapter, but the author recommends that whilst either design can be used for variable measures, for attribute measures the limits should be set up by use of the Poisson distribution and not the approximation of ± 3 standard deviations, since the normal distribution is only a reasonable approximation to the binomial when p is greater than 0.10 — a condition seldom met in quality control.

5.3   Attribute Control Charts

5.3.1   British Standard Attribute Control Charts

Attribute measures of quality are obtained by means of *go/no go* gauging or, if the product is classified either objectively or subjectively into acceptable or not.

Objective assessments include gauging to a standard, correct functioning of product, etc., whereas the assessment of satisfactory colour, appearance, surface finish, etc., of the product is subjective judgement of the individual inspector.

Having calculated the process capability, the data for maintaining control are obtained by taking samples at specified intervals and plotting the results on a control chart. There are two basic types of attribute control chart, the 'p' chart, or fraction defective, and the 'C' chart, the number of defects in the sample, and either can be used, depending on circumstances. The 'C' chart will be used throughout this book. The charts can also be adapted for variable sample sizes, although it is simpler to maintain the sample size constant.

Providing the process capability or standard is less than 0.10 fraction defective or 10% defective, then the Poisson distribution can be used to obtain the limits as an approximation to the binomial. The use of this Poisson approximation is widely used in the setting up of control charts.

The statistical tables (at the end of this book) contain a tabulation of the cumulative Poisson distribution (table 1*) for use in determining the control limits.

Before proceeding, three examples demonstrating the use of the Poisson tables are given:

(a) What is the chance of getting 2 or more successes in a Poisson process with mean number of successes 1.6?
Here $m = 1.6$.
From table 1*, probability of 2 or more successes = 0.4751.

(b) What is the probability of exactly 2 successes?
Here probability of 2 or more successes = 0.4751
and probability of 3 or more successes = 0.2166
∴ Probability of exactly 2 successes = 0.4751 − 0.2166
$$= 0.2585$$

(c) What is the probability of exactly 0 successes?
Probability of 0 or more = 1.0000
Probability of 1 or more = 0.7981
Probability of exactly 0 successes = 1.0000 − 0.7981 = 0.2019.

Example of the Setting up of an Attribute Control Chart

An automatic process has a process capability of 5% defective. Samples of size $n = 100$ are taken every half hour. Set up the Control Chart.
Here $n = 100$ $p_0 = 0.05$
The 'expected' or average defects per sample of 100, $np_0 = 100 \times 0.05 = 5.0$, if the process is operating at its standard. $\frac{c}{100} = 0.05$

It is necessary to calculate the control limits. In the case of attribute schemes it is usual only to specify the upper limits. However, where it is considered applicable, lower limits can also be calculated.

In this example the Poisson approximation to the binomial can be used.
Thus $m = np_0 = 100 \times 0.05 = 5.0$.

Now the tables have to be used in a slightly different manner. The questions now are, with the process in control at process capability of 5%, what are:

(1) the level of defects which have only a 1 in 40 chance of being exceeded in the random sample? - warning limit. And

(2) the level of defects which have only a 1 in 1000 chance of being exceeded in the random sample? - action limit.

From table 1* for $m = 5.0$. The probability of 10 defects or more (i.e. the probability of exceeding 9 defects) = 0.0318. The probability of 11 defects or more (i.e. the probability of exceeding 10 defects) = 0.0137.

Since the level of probability required is 0.025 (1 in 40), it is recommended that the figure nearest is taken. Thus the *warning limit* is set at 9, giving a 0.0318 chance of getting defects exceeding this in a sample of 100 if the process is in control; thus if a sample gives over 9 defects, it is a 'warning' or indication that process has gone out of control.

Table 1 also gives:

The probability of 13 defects or more (probability of exceeding 12 defects) = 0.0020.

The probability of 14 defects or more (probability of exceeding 13 defects) = 0.0007.

Again, taking the nearest value to 0.001 gives 13 defects/sample as the *action limit*. The logic of this being that if more than 13 defects are found in a sample of 100, then there is only a 0.0007 (approximation to 0.001) chance of this occurring if the process is in control, or this probability is so low that it can be

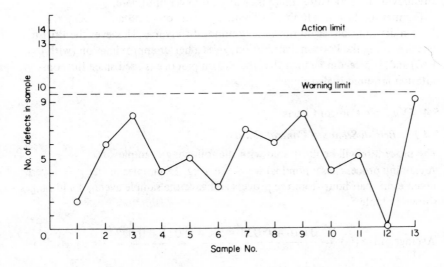

Figure 5.1 Attribute Control Chart (British Standard)

asserted that the process is out of control with only a 0.0007 chance of being wrong. This control chart is shown in figure 5.1, with the results of the last 13 samples plotted.

It is recommended that when plotting the control chart the limits are positioned at:

Warning limit draw at 9.5
Action limit draw at 13.5

This step removes the ambiguity which inevitably arises when points fall on the limits — here points are either inside or outside the limits. It will be noted that the warning limit is shown by a dotted line and the action limit by a full line.

Control is therefore maintained by taking samples of 100 and plotting the number of defectives on this chart — a point outside Warning Limited indicating that the process is not operating at its standard while a point outside the action limit almost certainly (only 1 - 1000 approximately of being wrong) showing process is out of control.

5.3.2 American Attribute Control Charts

The American practice has only one set of limits, the outer, and these limits are set at ± 3 standard deviations from process average.

Standard deviation of No. of defects in a sample $= \sqrt{np_0(1-p_0)}$

Thus limits are $np_0 \pm 3\sqrt{np_0(1-p_0)}$

So, using the same example as for the British charts, then $n = 100, p_0 = 0.05$
The limits are $np_0 \pm 3\sqrt{np_0(1-p_0)}$ $= 5 \pm 6.54$

Thus the outer limit is placed at 12 (nearest unit value and the limit is therefore drawn at 12.5). Note: there is clearly no lower limit here.

Comparing the outer limit of 12 with the value of 13 obtained using the Poisson distribution, again shows only minor differences. However the British practice, using the Poisson distribution, gives a better approximation (with $p < 0.10$) and, it is recommended that the British practice is used since the computation required is also simpler.

5.4 Variable Control Charts

5.4.1 British Standard Control Charts

The procedure will be illustrated with the following example:
A canning process has a nominal weight of 1 kg, 25 samples of size $n = 4$ were taken every half hour from the process and gave the sample averages and ranges shown in table 5.1.

$$\text{Average range } (\bar{w}) = \frac{0.016 + 0.028 + \ldots + 0.021 + 0.028}{25}$$

$$= 0.020 \text{ kg}$$

Table 5.1

Sample No.	1	2	3	4	5	6	7	8	9	10
Sample average ($\bar{X}$)	1.003	1.007	1.005	1.005	0.998	0.988	1.001	0.999	1.004	0.992
Sample range (w)	0.016	0.028	0.014	0.035	0.018	0.028	0.022	0.010	0.027	0.041
Sample No.	11	12	13	14	15	16	17	18	19	20
Sample average ($\bar{X}$)	0.995	0.998	1.002	1.000	0.998	0.994	1.008	1.002	1.001	0.999
Sample range (w)	0.020	0.016	0.009	0.005	0.025	0.008	0.024	0.002	0.018	0.008
Sample No.	21	22	23	24	25					
Sample average ($\bar{X}$)	1.003	0.998	1.006	1.000	1.002					
Sample range (w)	0.025	0.017	0.031	0.021	0.028					

Therefore Process capability $\sigma_0 = \dfrac{\bar{w}}{d_n}$ (for $n = 4, d_n = 2.059$ from table 6*)

$$= \frac{0.020}{2.059} = 0.0097 \simeq 0.010 \text{ kg}$$

Thus when process is in control the container weights will be within $\pm 1.96 \times 0.01$ kg or ± 0.0196 kg with 95% confidence.

Process Average Control Limits   ẍ chart

Warning Limits. Thus, for only a 1 in 40 chance of an average falling outside if process is in *control,* limits are

$$\text{Process average} \pm 1.96 \frac{\sigma_0}{\sqrt{n}}$$

Action Limits. Similarly, action limits are

$$\text{Process average} \pm 3.09 \frac{\sigma_0}{\sqrt{n}} \text{ for a 1 in 1000 chance of falling outside either}$$

the upper or lower limit.
Thus the limits for this process are

$$\text{Warning limits} = 1 \pm 1.96 \frac{0.01}{\sqrt{4}} = 1 \pm 0.0098 \doteqdot 1 \pm 0.010 \text{ kg}$$

$$\text{Action limits} = 1 \pm 3.09 \frac{0.01}{\sqrt{4}} = 1 \pm 0.0154 \doteqdot 1 \pm 0.015 \text{ kg}$$

However in practice it is easier and simpler to read directly from table 4* the multiplying factors for obtaining the limits. Thus from table 4* for $n=4$, multiply σ_0 by 0.98 for warning limits and by 1.545 for the action limits giving directly the limits already obtained.

Again there is no need in practice to calculate σ_0, although it is usual to do so, since the limits can also be obtained directly from the average range $\bar{w}$ by the multiplying factors $A^1_{0.0025}$ (warning limit) and $A^1_{0.001}$ (action limit).

Thus the warning limits = $1 \pm 0.02 \times 0.476 = 1 \pm 0.0095$ kg as before; and, action limits = $1 \pm 0.02 \times 0.75 = 1 \pm 0.015$ kg as before.

Range Control Limits

With variables, in addition to the control chart for the process average, a control chart is also required for the process variation to detect if this variation goes out of control.

For simplicity and as specified by British standards, the control is placed on the sample range.

Tables 5* or 6* give the multiplying factors for the range chart. In practice usually only upper limits are employed.

Thus from table 5* $\overline{w}$

Upper warning limit = 1.93 × 0.02 = 0.038 kg
Upper action limit = 2.57 × 0.02 = 0.054 kg

or from table 6* σ

Upper warning limit = 3.98 × 0.01 = 0.039 kg
Upper action limit = 5.30 × 0.01 = 0.053 kg

The slight difference being due to the rounding off errors in calculating the standard deviation (σ_0).

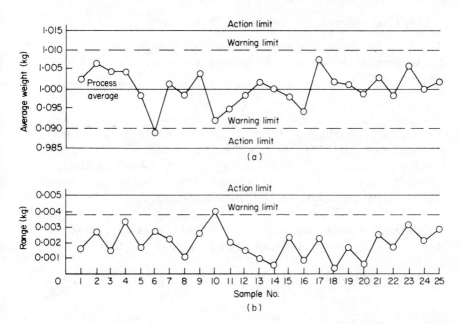

Figure 5.2 (a) Process average chart (b) Range chart (British Standard)

Figure 5.2 gives these control charts together with the results of 25 samples. When the samples are plotted, the plot should be examined for evidence of out of control — points outside the limits.

Control is maintained by taking samples of size $n=4$ at regular intervals, plotting the sample average ($\overline{X}$) and range (w) on the control chart.

5.4.2   *American Practice*
Process Average Charts

The control charts for the process average contain only outer limits set at $\pm 3\sigma_0/\sqrt{n}$.

Again as with British standard charts, multipliers are tabulated to enable limits to be calculated directly from the average range $(\bar{w})$.

Thus upper control limit $= \bar{X} + A_2 \bar{w}$
     Lower control limit $= \bar{X} - A_2 \bar{w}$.

The values of the multipliers A_2 are given in table 7* in the appendix.

Range Charts

For range charts, 3 sigma limits are again used. The standard deviation of the range is calculated and the upper and lower limits are calculated as

$$\bar{w} \pm 3\sigma_w, \text{ where } \sigma_w = \text{ standard deviation of range}$$

As with the British charts, multipliers are tabulated enabling limits to be obtained directly from the average range. The multipliers are also tabulated in table 7* for $n = 2$ to $n = 12$.

   Lower limit $= D_3 \bar{w}$ Upper limit $= D_4 \bar{w}$

   Comparing the multipliers for British charts (table 4*) with those of the American charts (table 7*), shows that the outer probability limits used in British charts are outside the American 3 sigma limits. However, as stated, the probability values are arbitrary and since the differences are not great, clearly it does not matter significantly which chart design is used.

   Consider an example used for British charts in Section 5.4.1, page 40. Here $\bar{w} = 0.02$ kg. Sample size $n = 4$. Process capability $\sigma_0 = 0.01$ kg.

American Chart Design

Process Average Chart

$$\text{Limits} = \bar{X} \pm 3 \frac{\sigma_0}{\sqrt{n}}$$

$$= \bar{X} \pm 3 \times \frac{0.01}{\sqrt{4}} = \bar{X} \pm 0.015$$

From table 7*

$$\text{Limits} = \bar{X} \pm A_2 \bar{w}$$

$$= \bar{X} \pm 0.729 \times 0.02$$

$$= \bar{X} \pm 0.0146 \doteq \bar{X} \pm 0.015$$

the same as before.

Range Chart From table 7*
Upper limit $= D_4 \bar{w}$

$$= 2.282 \times 0.02$$

$$\doteq 0.05$$

Note: there is no lower limit available here.

Thus the limits obtained here are approximately the same as for British standard practice. The design which is chosen is simply a matter of individual choice.

In the case of variable measures, the differences between the British and American practice are minor – the British using two limits, the Americans only the outer limits. Clearly whichever design is chosen is simply a matter of personal choice.

The British practice has been adopted throughout this book, but readers who wish to use the American chart design should work out examples using this design.

5.5 Sensitivity of Charts at Detecting Changes in Process Average

In the design of control charts, the question 'How effective is the chart at detecting any given change in the process average?' or the definition of a suitable 'measure of effectiveness' for control charts is fundamental to their understanding.

The measure adopted here is the average run length to detection (A.R.L.), that is, for any given change in the process average, the number of samples which are required on the average to detect this change – detection being defined as a point outside the limits – in the case of British charts where there are two limits, the *action limit* is used for detection.

5.5.1 *Relationship between A.R.L. and the Probability of a Point Falling outside the Limit*

If the probability of a sample being *out* of *control* $= p_1$
then:
Probability of *out* of *control* in 1st sample $= p_1$
Probability of *out* of *control* not being detected until the 2nd sample $= (1-p_1)p_1$
etc.

Probability of *out* of *control* not being detected until the ith sample
$= (1-p_1)^{i-1}p_1$
Therefore average number of samples till detection (A.R.L.)

$$= \sum_{i=1}^{\infty} i\,(1-p_1)^{i-1}p_1$$

A.R.L. $= 1p_1 + 2p_1\,(1-p_1) + 3p_1\,(1-p_1)^2 + \ldots$
$ = p_1\,|1 + 2(1-p_1) + 3(1-p_1)^2 + \ldots|$

$$\text{A.R.L.} = \frac{p_1}{|1-(1-p_1)|^2} = \frac{1}{p_1}$$

5.5.2 Calculation of A.R.L.s

Attribute Charts

Consider the example in Section 5.3.1 (page 38). Here process capability $p_0 = 0.05$. Sample size $n = 100$ taken every half hour. Warning limit $= 9$; action limit $= 13$. Out of control is detected by a sample point outside the action limit of 13.

What is the A.R.L. if process average changes to:

(i)   10% defective
(ii)   8% defective
(iii)   6% defective?

(i) 10% defective: $m = np = 100 \times 0.10 = 10.0$
Probability of getting more than 13 defects $= 0.1355$ (from table 1*)

Therefore A.R.L. $= \dfrac{1}{0.1355} = 7.38$ or 7.38 samples will be required on the

average to detect the change to 10% defective.

(ii) 8% defective: $m = np = 100 \times 0.08 = 8.0$
Probability of getting more than 13 defects $= 0.0342$

Therefore A.R.L. $= \dfrac{1}{0.0342} = 29.2$ samples

(iii) 6% defective: $m = np = 100 \times 0.06 = 6.0$
Probability of getting more than 13 defects $= 0.0036$

Therefore A.R.L. $= \dfrac{1}{0.0036} = 277.8$ samples

Variable Charts

Consider the example given in Section 5.4.1, page 40,
Outer control limits $= \overline{X} \pm 0.015$ kg $= 1.00 \pm 0.015$ kg

Consider now the A.R.L. required to detect the following changes in process average:

(i)   Process average changes to 1.010 kg.
(ii)   Process average changes to 1.005 kg.
(iii) Process average changes to 1.002 kg.

(i)   Process average = 1.01 kg (see figure 5.3).

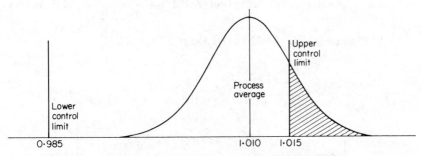

Figure 5.3 Distribution of sample average

$$U = \frac{1.015 - 1.010}{0.010/ \sqrt{4}} = 1.0 \quad \text{Area outside upper limit} = 0.1587$$

$$U = \frac{0.985 - 1.010}{0.010/ \sqrt{4}} = 5.0 \quad \text{Area outside lower limit} = \text{neg}$$

Therefore probability of sample point falling outside outer control limits = 0.1587

Therefore average number of samples to detect change (A.R.L.) $= \dfrac{1}{0.1587}$

$$= 6.3 \text{ samples}$$

(ii) Process average = 1.005 kg (see figure 5.4).

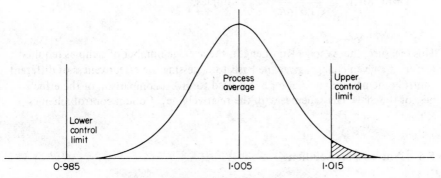

Figure 5.4 Distribution of sample average

$$U = \frac{1.015 - 1.005}{0.010/\sqrt{4}} = 2.0 \text{ Area outside upper limit} = 0.02275$$

$$U = \frac{0.985 - 1.005}{0.010/\sqrt{4}} = 4.0 \text{ Area outside lower limit} = \text{neg.}$$

Therefore probability of a point outside outer control limits = 0.02275

Therefore average run length to detection (A.R.L.) = $\dfrac{1}{0.02275}$ = 44.0 samples

(iii) Process average = 1.002 kg (see figure 5.5).

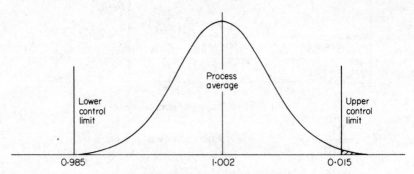

Figure 5.5 Distribution of sample average

$$U = \frac{1.015 - 1.002}{0.010/\sqrt{4}} = 2.6 \text{ Area outside upper limit} = 0.00466$$

$$U = \frac{0.985 - 1.002}{0.010/\sqrt{4}} = 3.4 \text{ Area outside lower limit} = \text{neg.}$$

Therefore probability of a point outside control limits = 0.00466

Therefore A.R.L. = $\dfrac{1}{0.00466}$ = 215 samples.

5.5.3 Summary

This measure, the Average Run Length, the average number of samples required to detect a given change, gives the basis for assessing the effectiveness of different control schemes and in Chapter 8 it is used to give a comparison of the effectiveness of the Shewhart schemes with the relatively new CuSum control schemes (Chapters 6 and 7).

5.6 Problems for Solution

N.B. The British practice has been adopted in all problems. Readers who wish to use the American type charts, should solve the problems using the American design.

Again, as stated in Chapter 4, the number of samples has in some cases been reduced below 25, to simplify the computation.

No. 1

Question (1), Section 4.5, page 29. Set up control chart for this process.

No. 2

Question (2), Section 4.5, page 29. Set up control chart for this process.

If process average changes to 3% defective, what is the A.R.L. for detecting this change?

No. 3

The expenditure on tooling per month by a firm is:

1	£2610
2	£3080
3	£2765
4	£2800
5	£2950
6	£3210
7	£2875
8	£3100
9	£2785
10	£2920

(Assume that production requirements call for an expected equal expenditure per month.)

Set up control chart for this operation.

No. 4

In the growing of cotton, if more than 1 plant in 20 (5%) is infested, then the crop should be sprayed with insecticide.

The standard level of infestation is 2%, at which level spraying should not occur.

Assuming that infection is randomly distributed and samples are taken every week, calculate the sample size n and set up the Shewhart chart to detect when to spray, such that a 5% infestation rate will be detected in 3 samples on the average. (Detection defined as a point outside *action* limit.)

No. 5

25 samples of size 50 gave the following number of defects from a production process:

0	1	0	2	0
2	0	2	0	1
0	0	1	0	0
1	0	0	1	0
0	1	0	2	0

Set up the control chart for the process.

If the defective rate doubles, what is the average number of samples needed to detect this change?

No. 6

(i) The average range of 25 samples of size $n = 6$ taken from a process was $\bar{w} = 0.04$ kg. What is the process capability? Set up the Shewhart control chart.

(ii) If the process goes *out of control* by $+0.01$ kg, what is the probability of detecting this change in the next three samples?

No. 7

The process capability of a process is 6% defective. It has now gone out of control and is producing at 8.4% defective. If the sample size is $n = 100$, what is the probability that at least one of the next two samples plotted on the Shewhart control chart will be out of control?

No. 8

The process capability of a process producing rivets is 0.10 mm. If the nominal dimension is 10 mm, set up the Shewhart control chart for the process. Sample size $n = 5$.

If the process average drifts to 10.10 mm, what is the probability that a sample will detect this change?

No. 9

Given that the cost of Inspecting is £S per 100 and that the process capability of the process is p_0. If the cost of not detecting an out of control condition of $(p_0 + a)\%$ is £La per 1000 produced and given the production rate as 5000/h, discuss the setting up of a formula for:

(a) optimum sample size (n); and
(b) optimum interval between samples.

5.7 Solutions to Problems

No. 1

Here $\bar{w} = 0.151$ mm

$$\sigma_0 = \frac{0.151}{2.847} = 0.053 \text{ mm}$$

Control limits for process average from table 4*

Warning limits = process average $\pm 0.693 \times 0.053 = \bar{X} + 0.037$ mm
Action limits = process average $\pm 1.092 \times 0.053 = \bar{X} \pm 0.061$ mm

Control limits for sample range from table 6*.

Upper warning limit = 4.61 × 0.053 = 0.244 mm
Upper action limit = 5.80 × 0.053 = 0.307 mm

The assumption that the process is in control is checked by plotting sample results on the control chart and studying the pattern and number of points outside the limits.

No. 2

Here Process capability $p_0 = 0.021$
Sample size $n = 100$
Average number of defects/sample $m = np = 100 \times 0.21 = 2.1$

From table 1*

Warning limit = 5.5   Giving a probability of 0.0204 of being exceeded if process is in control.

Action limit = 7.5   Giving a probability of 0.0015 of being exceeded if process is in control.

If process average changes to 0.03, then

$$m = np = 100 \times 0.03 = 3.0$$

Probability of a sample point falling outside action limit = 0.0119 (from table 1*)

$$\text{Then A.R.L.} = \frac{1}{0.0119} = 84 \text{ samples}$$

No. 3

Here the sample size $n = 1$.

The number of readings is too small to carry out anything other than a visual check on the distribution of monthly overheads.

There is no evidence from this to suggest out of control.

Since $n = 1$, the range conversion cannot be used to calculate the standard deviation.

Calculate process capability σ_0 as

$$\sigma_0 = \sqrt{\frac{\Sigma(x_i - \bar{x})^2}{n-1}} = \sqrt{\frac{\Sigma x_i^2 - \dfrac{(\Sigma x_i)^2}{n}}{(n-1)}}$$

$$= 181$$

Thus control limits for expenditure:

Warning limits $= \bar{X} \pm 1.96 \times 181 = \bar{X} \pm 355$

$\qquad\qquad = \bar{X} \pm 3.09 \times 181 = \bar{X} \pm 560$

Average expenditure $= £2910$

There is clearly no range control chart.

No. 4

Let n = sample size. Let A = action limit. Then when $m_2 = 0.05 \times n$, the probability of a point outside A is 0.3333. Also when $m = 0.02 \times n$, the probability of a point outside A is 0.001.

The value of n can best be obtained by iteration.

Let $n = 100$, then $m_1 = 2$

$\qquad\qquad\qquad m_2 = 5$

For $m_1 = 2$, the action limit $A = 7.5$ (from table 1*)
For $m_2 = 5$, the probability of a point outside $A = 0.1334$ (from table 1*) which is less than the required value of 0.33.

Therefore increase $n = 160$ $m_1 = 3.2$

$\qquad\qquad\qquad\qquad\qquad m_2 = 8.0$

Action limit $A = 10.5$

For $m_2 = 8.0$, probability of a point outside $A = 0.184$ – which is still too low.

Therefore increase n to 200, $m_1 = 4$

$\qquad\qquad\qquad\qquad\qquad m_2 = 10$

Here action limit $A = 11.5$.

For $m_2 = 10$, probability of a point outside $A = 0.3032$ (which is now close to required value of 0.33).

Therefore increase n slightly to 210, $m_1 = 4.2$

$\qquad\qquad\qquad\qquad\qquad\qquad m_2 = 10.5$

Action limit $A = 11.5$

For $m_2 = 10.5$, probability of point outside $A \doteqdot 0.36$ (interpolated from table 1*).

Thus the solution is a sample size of between $n = 200$ and $n = 210$ – in practice, $n = 200$ would be accurate enough.

Thus limits are drawn at:

Warning limit (1/40) $= 8.5$
Action limit (1/1000) $= 11.5$

No. 5

To test hypothesis that process is in control (table 5.2).

Table 5.2

No. of defects	0	1	2	Total
Frequency	15	6	4	25
Poisson probability	0.55	0.33	0.12	1.00
Poisson frequency	13.7	8.8	3	24.9

$$\text{Average number of defects} = \frac{15 \times 0 + 6 \times 1 + 4 \times 2}{25} = \frac{14}{25} = 0.56 \doteq 0.60$$

The χ^2 test cannot be applied as there are not sufficient degrees of freedom. However, there is clearly no evidence of *out of control*.
For $m = 0.60$ (from table 1*)
Warning limit = 2.5
Action limit = 4.5
If defect rate doubles, average defects/sample $m = 1.2$
Therefore probability of exceeding 4 defects in sample = 0.0077

$$\text{Therefore A.R.L.} = \frac{1}{0.0077} = 130 \text{ samples}$$

No. 6

(1) Here, average range $\bar{w} = 0.04$ kg, and sample size $n = 6$.
Then from table 6*

$$\text{Process capability } \sigma_0 = \frac{0.04}{d_n} = \frac{0.04}{2.534} = 0.0158 \text{ kg}$$

Control limits for Shewhart control chart are obtained as follows.
For process average (from table 4*)

Warning limits = Process average $\pm 0.316 \times 0.04$
= Process average ± 0.013 kg

Action limit = Process average $\pm 0.498 \times 0.04$
= Process average ± 0.02 kg

For range (from table 5*)
Upper warning limit = $1.72 \times 0.04 = 0.07$ kg
Upper action limit = $2.21 \times 0.04 = 0.09$ kg

(2) Let unknown process average = $\bar{X}$ kg
then new process average = $\bar{X} + 0.01$ kg, upper action limit = $\bar{X} \pm 0.02$ kg (see figure 5.6).

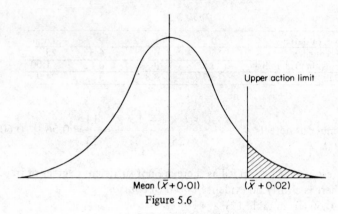

Figure 5.6

Mean $= \overline{X} + 0.01$

$$U = \frac{(\overline{X} + 0.02) - (\overline{X} + 0.01)}{\dfrac{0.0158}{\sqrt{6}}} = \frac{0.01 \times \sqrt{6}}{0.0158} = 1.55 \ \text{(from table 2*)}$$

Note. The probability of getting a point outside the lower limit can be ignored.

From table 2*, the probability of a sample average exceeding the upper action limit = 0.0606

Therefore probability of at least one point being outside action limit in next three samples = 1 − (probability of no point outside)

$$= 1 - (1 - 0.0606)^3$$
$$= 0.171$$

or a 17.1% chance of detecting change inside three samples.

No. 7

Here the process capability $(p) = 0.06$. Thus average defects/sample $m = np$ $= 100 \times 0.06 = 6.0$ (from table 1*).

Warning limit = 11 (probability of exceeding = 0.0201)
Action limit = 14 (probability of exceeding = 0.0014)
or Action limit = 15 (probability of exceeding = 0.0005).

Choose action limit as 14 since the probability of exceeding the limit is closer to the theoretical value 0.001.

Defining *out of control* on the chart as a point outside the *action limit*, if $p = 0.084$ then $m = np = 100 \times 0.084 = 8.4$.

Therefore from table 1* with $m = 8.4$,
probability of a point above 14 = 0.0251

Therefore probability that at least one of the next two points is out of control
= 1−(probability that no point is out of control)
= $1 - (1 - 0.0251)^2$
= $1 - (0.9749)^2$
= 0.025% or 2.5%

Thus, there is only approximately a 2.5% chance of detecting the change in process average from 6% to 8.4% in the next two samples of size 100.

No. 8

Process capability σ_0 = 0.10 mm, sample size n = 5, nominal dimension = 10 mm. From table 4* in Appendix,
Warning limits = 10 mm ± 0.876 × 0.10 mm
$\qquad\qquad\quad$ = 10 ± 0.0876 mm
Action limits $\;$ = 10 ± 1.382 × 0.10 mm
$\qquad\qquad\quad$ = 10 ± 0.138 mm
If process average changes to 10.10 mm, what is the probability now of a sample average falling outside the action limits?

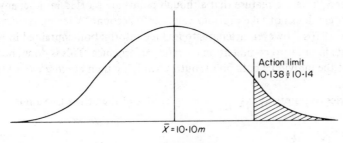

Figure 5.7

Clearly it is only necessary to consider the upper limit.

$$\text{Therefore } U = \frac{10.14 - 10.10}{\dfrac{0.10}{\sqrt{5}}} = \frac{0.04 \times \sqrt{5}}{0.10} = 0.894 \doteqdot 0.89$$

Therefore from table 2*, probability of a point outside the *action limit* = 0.1867

Therefore probability of a given sample of size 5 detecting the change = 0.1867 ≑ 0.19

No. 9

It is not possible to give an ideal solution here, but students should be able at least to understand the inter-relationship of the factors involved. Students on advanced courses should make an attempt to construct a model.

This problem contains the crux of the decisions facing all practical quality controllers when installing a quality control system and yet, surprisingly, is usually not covered in text books.

Tutors should lead a discussion period on this problem at some stage in the training of quality controllers.

6. Introduction to Cumulative Sum Charts

6.1 Introduction

Conventional charting techniques, such as the Shewhart control charts, described in Chapter 5, have the feature that although points are plotted in time, any testing done on them does not take previous values into account. A technique developed in the late 1950s, however, attempts to include information contained in past data points in order to comment on current performance. This is done, not by looking at the individual data point, but by studying their *cumulative sums* or *'cusum'*.

If a series of points $x_1, x_2 \ldots$ is being produced then their CuSum is developed as follows:

$$S_1 = (x_1 - k)$$

$$S_2 = (x_1 - k) + (x_2 - k) = S_1 + (x_2 - k)$$

.

.

.

.

$$S_r = \sum_{i=1}^{r} (x_i - k) = S_{r-1} + (x_r - k)$$

where k is a constant called the *Reference Value*, If the CuSums, S_r, are calculated and plotted as they occur, a 'CuSum chart' is produced.

The constant k may be any value, even zero, but in order to save the chart running off the edge of the paper it is usually set at about the expected mean value of the data points. Again this implies setting k near to the standard of the process.

If the mean value of the process increases, however, there will be a general rise in the level of the CuSum as more and more $(x_i - k)$ values are at a positive level. Similarly, should the mean decrease, the graph begins to slope downwards.

56

In fact a *change of mean* in the original series becomes a *change of slope* in the CuSum. The actual level of the CuSum at any point is immaterial. In practice, because of the small random fluctuations in most processes, there will be small deviations in the slope of a CuSum chart and it is usual to look at the average slope of a number of points to see if any change in level has occurred.

The CuSum charts are also more general than the Shewhart charts in that control can be achieved by individual readings (i.e. sample size $n = 1$). This fact, that the CuSum can in many cases give a basis for control on individual readings, makes it ideally suitable for process control where the production rate is relatively low or where cost of inspection is high. Also, as will be demonstrated here and more fully in the next two chapters, CuSum charts are more effective than Shewhart charts in detecting small changes in the Process Average.

6.2   The CuSum Chart

The plotting of a CuSum chart will now be demonstrated.

Consider again the data on machine breakdowns per week, given in problem 3 page 26 (see table 6.1).

Table 6.1

Week No.	No. of breakdowns per week									
1 – 10	0	4	3	6	2	0	1	1	0	1
11 – 20	1	3	0	0	3	0	5	0	0	1
21 – 30	0	1	4	2	0	1	5	0	5	6
31 – 40	4	1	5	0	2	4	4	1	1	0
41 – 50	5	2	0	1	1	5	0	4	0	5

Figure 6.1 shows the conventional graph of the plot of the number of breakdowns.

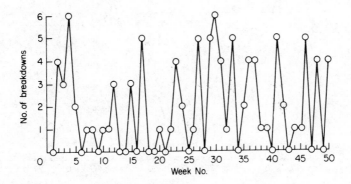

Figure 6.1 Number of breakdowns

There is no apparent evidence of any change in the breakdown rate — the large variation makes it difficult to detect any change.

The CuSum will now be calculated. The first step is to select a value of k, the reference value. As stated in previous section, the reference value (k) can be any value. However, since the use of the CuSum here is as a visual aid to detecting changes in the variable and thus diagnosing causes for this change, the selection of the reference value (k) should be chosen near the process average since this high-lights the visual presentation of changes in the variable.

The average breakdowns/week = 2.0

Thus, let the reference value (k) = 2.0

Note. To simplify the computation of the CuSum, the reference value (k) should always be taken as a round number i.e. if average breakdowns here had been 2.2, the reference value (k) would still be taken as 2.0 (see examples in Section 6.3).

The values of the CuSum are shown in table 6.2.

Table 6.2

Sample No.				CuSum values $$S_n = \sum_{i=1}^{n} (x_i - 2)$$					
1 – 10	−2	0	+1	+5	+5	+3	+2	+1	−1	−2
11 – 20	−3	−2	−4	−6	−5	−7	−4	−6	−8	−9
21 – 30	−11	−12	−10	−10	−12	−13	−10	−12	−9	−5
31 – 40	−3	−4	−1	−3	−3	−1	+1	0	−1	−3
41 – 50	0	0	−2	−3	−4	−1	−3	−1	−3	0

This CuSum plot is shown in figure 6.2.

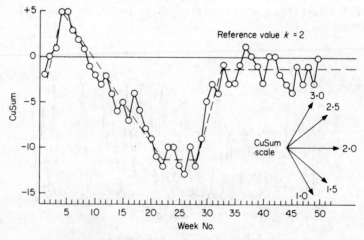

Figure 6.2 CuSum of number of breakdowns/week

The scale of the CuSum chart is shown in figure 6.2. It should be noted that it is the *slope* of the graph which measures the variate value — thus here, if graph is horizontal (or zeroslope) the system is running at an average of 2.0 breakdowns/ wk; again if the average breakdown rate increases to 3.0 per week then the CuSum will gain the average + 1 units of CuSum for every sample — thus, the CuSum will slope upwards — the slope being calculated as follows — for every 5 samples, an increase of + 5 CuSum units is obtained, etc.

Referring to figure 6.2, the chart shows that the breakdown rate has been changing over the year.

Diagnostically, for the 1st 4 weeks Average Breakdowns = 3.0/wk
$\qquad$ 5th — 22nd weeks Average Breakdowns = 1.0/wk
$\qquad$ 23rd — 28th weeks Average Breakdowns = 2.0/wk
$\qquad$ 29th — 33rd weeks Average Breakdowns = 4.0/wk
$\qquad$ 34th — 50th weeks Average Breakdowns = 2.0/wk

This example shows clearly the power of the CuSum in diagnosing the changes that have occurred. However, since this method is extremely sensitive to changes, care should be taken that changes in the breakdown rate are, wherever possible, linked to actual changes in practice.

6.3 Examples Illustrating the CuSum Chart

In the previous section, the CuSum chart, as a visual method of detecting when changes have occurred in the variable, was demonstrated. The CuSum chart thus gives a basis for relating these 'apparent' changes to changes which have occurred in practice or 'diagnosing'. However, it must be stressed again here that it is this extreme sensitivity of the CuSum which in itself can be misleading and visual apparent changes can arise due to random fluctuations in the variate. Thus, whenever possible, the significance of any change should be examined (see Chapter 7) but if care is exercised, management has a powerful diagnostic tool in the CuSum chart.

Since the CuSum as a diagnostic management tool has a wider field of application than process control, a series of examples have been chosen to illustrate the use of the CuSum as a diagnostic tool, not only from the field of process control but also from general management statistics.

Example No. 1: Process Control — The Zinc Coating of Galvanised Iron

In the control of the zinc coating process on galvanised iron, the average weight of the zinc coating (determined by a chemical method) for 25 samples of size $n = 5$ taken daily are given in table 6.3. These data are shown plotted in a conventional graph in figure 6.3.

Table 6.3

Sample No.	Aver. wt. of zinc coating (g)				
1 – 5	1.47	1.52	1.55	1.38	1.64
6 – 10	1.63	1.53	1.60	1.32	1.70
11 – 15	1.60	1.51	1.32	1.47	1.45
16 – 20	1.44	1.48	1.55	1.57	1.56
21 – 25	1.65	1.53	1.34	1.49	1.54

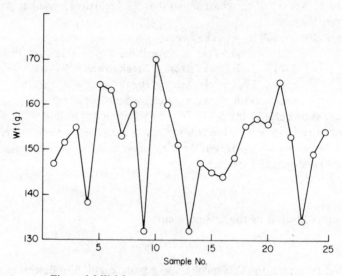

Figure 6.3 Weight of zinc coatings (conventional chart)

Calculation of CuSum

With reference value $k = 1.5$ the CuSum values for the data are given in table 6.4. Figure 6.4 gives the CuSum plot together with the CuSum scale. The dotted lines give the visual interpretation of apparent changes in the variate as:

Samples No.   1 – 12 – Average wt of zinc coating was 1.55 g
      13 – 17 – Average wt of zinc coating was 1.44 g
      18 – 20 – Average wt of zinc coating was 1.58 g
      21 – 25 – Average wt of zinc coating was 1.43 g

Table 6.4

Sample No.	CuSum values $|\Sigma(x_i - 1.5)|$				
1 – 5	−0.03	−0.01	+0.04	−0.08	+0.06
6 – 10	+0.19	+0.22	+0.32	+0.20	+0.40
11 – 15	+0.50	+0.51	+0.33	+0.30	+0.25
16 – 20	+0.19	+0.17	+0.22	+0.29	+0.35
21 – 25	+0.50	+0.53	+0.37	+0.36	+0.40

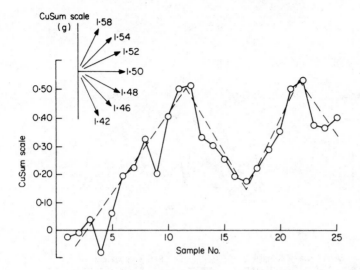

Figure 6.4 Weight of zinc coatings (CuSum chart)

Thus the CuSum has shown that this data consists of two heterogeneous groups, samples 1 – 12 and 18 – 20 with a process average between 1.55 and 1.58 g, and samples 13 – 17 and 21 – 25 with a process average of between 1.43 and 1.44 g.

Example No. 2: Process Control – Bolt Production

Table 6.5 gives the number of defects found in 25 samples of size $n = 100$ from a production process. This data is shown plotted in conventional form in figure 6.5 (a). Figure 6.5 (b) shows the CuSum chart for the data with reference value $k = 2$.

Table 6.5 No. of defects per sample (sample size n = 6)

Batch No.					
1 – 5	1	2	3	0	1
6 – 10	0	0	0	2	1
11 – 15	0	1	1	3	0
16 – 20	3	3	4	1	1
21 – 25	4	4	4	0	2

Here, the change in the defect rate of the process is so marked that the conventional chart does indicate the change – it is interesting to note however that the Shewhart control chart would not detect the change, i.e. no points outside *action limits.*

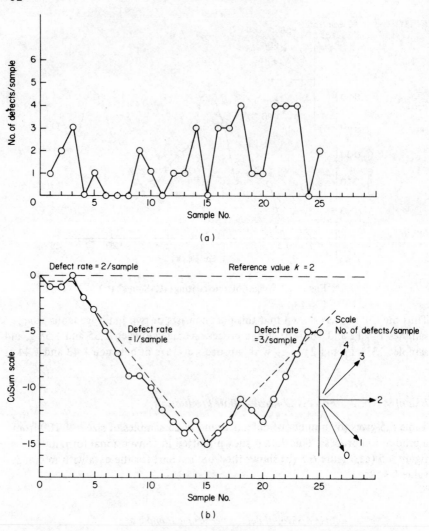

Figure 6.5 Number of defects per sample. (a) Conventional chart (b) CuSum chart

However, the change is again demonstrated much more clearly with the CuSum chart.

The changes diagnosed are as follows.

Process defect rate was approx. 2% over 1st — 3rd samples.
Change (1):
Process defect rate was changed to 1% over 4th — 15th samples.
Change (2):
Process defect rate was changed to 3% over last 10 samples.

Example No.3: Management Control – Audience Rating for Television Programme 'Panorama'

Table 6.6 gives the weekly audience rating for the programme 'Panorama' from week No.50 in 1970 to week No.50 in 1973 inclusive. The data is shown plotted in conventional form in figure 6.6 (a).

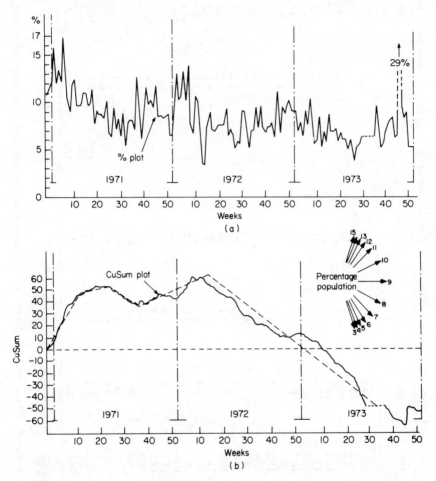

Figure 6.6 'Panorama' audience for each edition expressed as a percentage of population. (a) Conventional chart (b) CuSum chart

With reference value $k = 9\%$, the CuSum values of the data were calculated and the CuSum is shown plotted in figure 6.6 (b) together with the CuSum scale.

N.B. Missing readings are treated simply as having a value equal to the reference value (k), i.e. the CuSum is held at its current value for the period of missing readings.

Table 6.6 'Panorama' television programme – audience for each week's edition expressed as a percentage of the population

Week No.	1971 %	1972 %	1973 %	Week No.	1970 %	1971 %	1972 %	1973 %
1	15.9	9.9	X	27		9.5	5.2	5.3
2	12.0	13.3	7.0	28		7.1	5.9	5.5
3	13.7	10.4	8.1	29		8.4	5.4	6.4
4	12.1	10.9	6.4	30		6.3	9.2	X
5	17.1	13.5	9.1	31		9.2	9.1	X
6	12.8	10.3	7.5	32		5.4	7.6	X
7	10.5	14.1	10.4	33		7.9	5.2	X
8	9.2	7.5	7.2	34		8.2	7.1	X
9	11.9	6.7	5.7	35		X	X	X
10	12.6	10.9	6.0	36		7.2	9.6	9.7
11	9.7	10.3	8.5	37		12.9	7.3	7.1
12	9.7	7.1	5.3	38		8.7	9.7	5.3
13	10.1	3.5	7.1	39		6.2	7.5	5.9
14	11.0	X	5.7	40		9.2	6.9	7.1
15	X	7.5	8.8	41		11.7	7.5	7.9
16	9.5	9.0	7.0	42		9.8	7.4	8.5
17	10.0	7.3	X	43		10.3	8.0	8.6
18	11.5	7.0	7.4	44		9.5	6.2	6.3
19	7.9	7.4	5.9	45		11.9	11.4	6.6
20	9.4	7.7	6.9	46		8.5	6.7	24.9
21	8.8	7.7	6.1	47		8.7	9.6	9.5
22	X	X	X	48		8.4	8.8	8.4
23	8.5	9.5	5.1	49		8.6	9.7	9.1
24	10.3	6.5	6.3	50	10.8	8.8	10.8	9.1
25	6.7	7.2	5.0	51	11.5	6.6	9.1	5.4
26	6.3	6.6	3.8	52	12.3	X	X	

X = No reading available.

N.B. Where no reading is available the CuSum remains the same as the previous value and calculations continue as before.

Reference to the CuSum plot in figure 6.6 (b) shows that major changes have occurred over the period in the audience rating of the programme. The changes are shown by the dotted lines on the chart and are as follows:

Weeks

Initially   50 - 52 (1970)
            1 - 10 (1971)   Audience rating 12% on average initially.

1st change 11 – 24 (1971)   Audience rating changes to 9% on average.

2nd change 25 – 36 (1971)   Audience rating changes to 8.5% on average.

3rd change 37 - 52 (1971)
            1 - 11 (1972)   Audience rating changes to 10% on average.

4th change 12 - 52 (1972)
            1 - 30 (1973)   Audience rating changes to 8% on average.

5th change 30 onwards (1973) Audience rating changes to 9% on average.

Example No. 4: Process Control – Production of Dowel Pins

Table 6.7 gives the average size (mm) of samples of size $n = 10$ taken at regular intervals over a 2 hour production of Dowel Pins. The controlled dimension is 6.00 + 0.05 mm – 0.00 mm. The CuSum values are also given in table 6.7 with reference value $k = 6.01$.

Figure 6.7 gives the data charted in conventional form, while figure 6.8 gives the CuSum plot. The CuSum plot again gives a better diagnosis of changes to the process average.

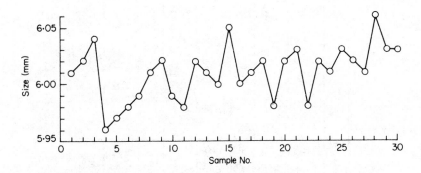

Figure 6.7 Production of dowel pins (Conventional chart)

Table 6.7

Sample No.	1	2	3	4	5	6	7	8	9	10
Sample average $\bar{X}_i$	6.01	6.02	6.04	5.96	5.97	5.98	5.99	6.01	6.02	5.99
CuSum $\Sigma(\bar{x}-6.01)$	0	0.01	0.03	-0.02	-0.06	-0.09	-0.11	-0.11	-0.1	-0.12
Sample No.	11	12	13	14	15	16	17	18	19	20
Sample average $\bar{X}_i$	5.98	6.02	6.01	6.00	6.05	6.00	6.01	6.02	5.98	6.02
CuSum $\Sigma(\bar{x}-6.01)$	-0.15	-0.14	-0.14	-0.5	-0.11	-0.12	-0.12	-0.11	-0.14	-0.13
Sample No.	21	22	23	24	25	26	27	28	29	30
Sample average $\bar{X}_i$	6.03	5.98	6.02	6.01	6.03	6.02	6.01	6.06	6.02	6.02
CuSum $\Sigma(\bar{X}_i-6.01)$	-0.11	-0.14	-0.13	-0.13	-0.11	-0.1	-0.1	-0.05	-0.04	-0.03

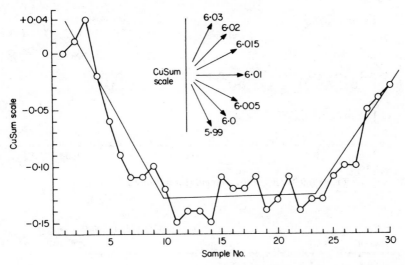

Figure 6.8 Production of dowel pins (CuSum chart)

Here changes occur:

For 1st 10 samples, process average is approx. 6.00 mm. For samples 11 - 22, process average is approx. 6.01 mm.
The U shape of figure 6.8 can also show that the mean value has been increasing steadily over the samples.

Example No. 5: Sales of all retail stores in U.S.A.

Table 6.8 gives the monthly sales in billions of dollars for all retail stores in the U.S.A. from 1951 to 1953.

Figure 6.9 gives the conventional plot of this data and while there is clear evidence of an increase in the last year, the CuSum plot in figure 6.10 shows what has happened far more clearly, namely half way through 1952 sales rate increased to £14 billion dollars per month.

Table 6.8 Total sales of retail stores (billions of dollars)

	Jan.	Feb.	Mar.	Apr.	May	June	July	Aug.	Sept.	Oct.	Nov.	Dec.
1951	13	12	13	13	13	13	12	13	13	14	13	15
1952	12	12	13	13	15	14	13	13	14	15	14	17
1953	13	12	14	14	15	15	14	14	14	15	14	16

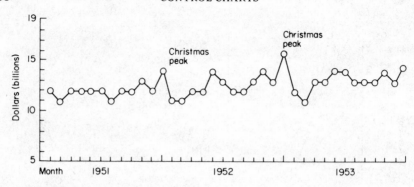

Figure 6.9 Total sales of all retail stores (Conventional chart)

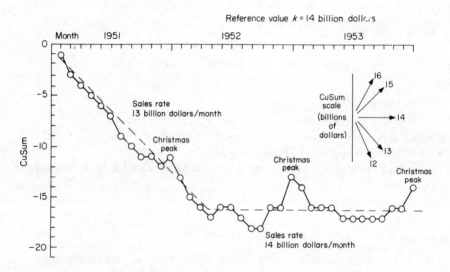

Figure 6.10 Total sales of all retail stores (CuSum chart)

Example No. 6: Case Study – Monitoring a Vehicle's Fuel Consumption

This case study, by my colleague J. A. Barnes of Cranfield is one of the best illustrations of the use of CuSum charts for monitoring data and is therefore given in full here.

The case study uses the double CuSum; that is a control chart where the 'time scale' is not in number of samples but where the 'time scale' incorporates variation; for example, here the 'time scale' is not the number of fill-ups, but the total gallons filled incorporating the fact that the number of gallons filled varies between fill-ups.

Table 6.9 Data for case study on fuel consumption

Date (1)	Speedometer reading (miles) (2)	Distance covered between fillings (3)	No. of gallons (into tank) (4)	Estimated consumption (miles/gallon) (5)	Total gallons put in (6)	CuSum (miles) (7)
19.11.66	12 180	94	4	23.50	4	−66
26.11	274	178	3	59.33	7	−8
28.11	452	163	3	54.33	10	35
1.12	615	75	3	25.00	13	−10
15.12	690	148	1	48.00	14	−2
17.12	738	61	2	30.50	16	−21
24.12	799	186	5	37.20	21	−35
30.12.66	12 985	63	4	15.75	25	−132
2.1.67	13 048	150	2	75.00	27	−62
7.1	198	119	4	29.75	31	−103
28.1	317	38	2	19.00	33	−145
4.2	355	125	3	41.66	36	−140
11.2	480	155	4	38.75	40	−145
15.2	635	124	4	31.00	44	−181
22.2	759	98	3	32.66	47	−203
25.2	857	74	2	37.00	49	−209
3.3	13 931	94	3	31.33	52	−235
11.3	14 025	46	2	23.00	54	−269
		Decoke, valves reground (two burnt out)				
18.3	051	111	4	27.75	58	−318
18.3	071	161	3	53.66	61	−277
24.3	182	137	3	45.66	64	−260
25.3	343	144	3	48.00	67	−236
27.3	480	147	3	49.00	70	−209
12.4	624	92	3	30.66	73	−237
13.4	771	48	3	49.33	76	−209
14.4	14 863					

Table 6.9 (continued)

Date (1)	Speedometer reading (miles) (2)	Distance covered between fillings (3)	No. of gallons (into tank) (4)	Estimated consumption (miles/gallon) (5)	Total gallons put in (6)	CuSum (miles) (7)
22.4	15 011	101	2	50.50	78	−188
3.5	112	159	4	39.75	82	−189
24.5	271	160	4	40.00	86	−189
2.6	431	161	4	40.25	90	−188
21.6	592	182	5	36.40	95	−206
1.7	774	128	3	42.66	98	−198
5.7	15 902	104	3	34.66	101	−214
6.7	16 006	195	2	97.50	103	−99
20.7	201	213	4	53.25	107	−46
2.8	414	67	3	22.33	110	−99
7.8	481	149	3	49.66	113	−70
19.8	630	157	4	39.25	117	−73
25.8	787	202	4	50.50	121	−31
4.9	16 989	67	2	33.50	123	−44
12.9	17 056	96	2	48.00	125	−28
13.9	095	New plugs; tappets, electrics checked				
17.9	152	192	5	38.40	130	−36
26.9	344	147	3	49.00	133	−9
6.10	491	167	4	41.75	137	−2
14.10	658	42	3	14.00	140	−80
21.10	700	206	4 FT	51.50	144	−34
28.10	17 906	211	4	52.75	148	−17
3.11	18 117	64	2	32.00	150	1
11.11	181	178	4	44.50	154	19
29.11	359	81	2	40.50	156	20
5.12	440	98	4	24.50	160	−42
13.12	538	109	2	54.50	162	−13
18.12	647	169	4	42.25	166	−4

Table 6.9 (continued)

Date (1)	Speedometer reading (miles) (2)	Distance covered between filling (3)	No. of gallons (into tank) (4)	Estimated consumption (miles/gallon) (5)	Total gallons put in (6)	CuSum (miles) (7)
23.12	816	158	3	52.66	169	34
31.12.67	18 974	168	4	42.00	173	42
6.1.68	19 142	155	4	38.75	177	37
27.1	297	131	4	32.75	181	8
3.2	428	116	2	58.00	183	44
9.2	544	126	4	31.50	187	10
29.2	619	Service, new brake linings, new contacts				
3.3	670	74	2	37.00	189	4
5.3	744	203	4	50.75	193	47
8.3	19 947	154	5	30.80	198	1
19.3	20 101	140	3	46.66	201	21
22.3	207	Two ZX tyres on front, SP41 on rear				
23.3	241	187	4	46.75	205	48
18.4	42	157	4	39.25	209	45
4.5	585	181	4	45.25	213	66
13.5	766	118	3	39.33	216	64
.5	20 844	164	4	41.00	220	68
4.6	21 048	141	4	35.25	224	49
16.6	189	169	4	42.25	228	58
4.7	358	139	4	34.75	232	37
14.7	497	222	4	55.50	236	99
19.7	660	New water pump, fan belt				
22.7	719	203	5	40.60	241	102
25.7	21 922	108	2	54.00	243	130
3.8	22 030	166	4	41.50	247	136
15.8	190	ZX tyres all wheels				
16.8	196	41	2	20.50	249	97
16.8	237	241	4 FT	60.25	253	178

Table 6.9 (continued)

Date	Speedometer reading (miles) (2)	Distance covered between fillings (3)	No. of gallons (into tank) (4)	Estimated consumption (miles/gallon) (5)	Total gallons put in (6)	CuSum (miles) (7)
19.8	478	163	4	40.75	257	181
22.8	641	240	4	60.00	261	261
24.8	22 881	222	5	44.40	266	283
31.8	23 103	171	4	42.75	270	294
14.9	274	125	5	25.00	275	159
21.9	339	150	2	75.00	277	289
25.9	549	244	5FT	48.80	282	333
30.9	793	109	3	36.33	285	322
11.10	23 902	138	4	34.50	289	300
22.10	24 040	55	2	27.50	291	275
26.10	095	172	3	57.33	294	327
2.11	267	152	5	30.40	299	279
9.11	419	152	2	76.00	301	351
12.11	571	123	3	41.00	304	354
26.11	694	81	2	40.50	306	355
3.12	775	71	2	35.50	308	346
8.12	846	132	2	66.00	310	398
12.12	24 978	132	4	33.00	314	370
14.12	25 110	153	2	76.50	316	443
17.12	263	142	4	35.50	320	425
30.12.68	405	200	5	40.00	325	425
15.1.69	605	202	4	50.50	329	467
23.1	25 807		3		332	

FT = Full tank.

In 1966, Barnes bought a second hand Singer Chamois car which had already covered 12 180 miles. Whenever petrol was put into the tank, a record was kept of (i) the date [col. (1)], (ii) the odometer reading, i.e. No. of miles on the clock [col. (2)], (iii) number of gallons filled [col. (4)].

These data are given in table 6.9, columns (1), (2) and (4); and column (6) gives the total gallons to date. Table 6.9. also contains details of maintenance and replacements made to the vehicle.

The vehicle's fuel consumption was then estimated by attributing the miles covered between successive fill-ups to the gallons filled, thus:

$$\text{Estimate of mpg at fill up } (i) = \frac{\begin{array}{c}\text{Odometer reading} \\ \text{at fill up } (i+1)\end{array} - \begin{array}{c}\text{Odometer reading} \\ \text{at fill up } (i)\end{array}}{\text{No. of gallons put in at } i\text{th fill up}}$$

Clearly these estimates are extremely poor, since they do not take into account changes in the level of fuel in the tank. These estimates are given in column (5) of table 6.9 and figure 6.11 gives their plot against total gallons used.

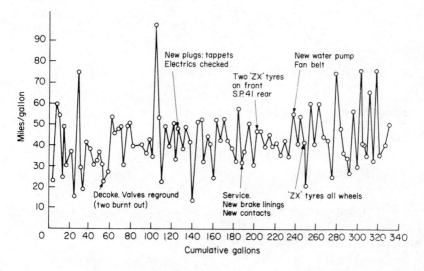

Figure 6.11 Singer Chamois: chart of fuel consumption

Individual estimates of mpg vary from 14.00 to 97.5 mpg and with such large errors their plot in figure 6.11 shows no evidence of any changes in fuel consumption over the period.

In practice some motorists attempt to reduce these large measurement errors, by errors, their plot in figure 6.11 shows no evidence of any changes in fuel con-

totalling miles covered and gallons used. This 'cumulative' estimate is shown plotted in figure 6.12.

While this 'cumulative' estimate does give a more accurate estimate of overall fuel consumption, it is almost insensitive to detecting any change in fuel consumption.

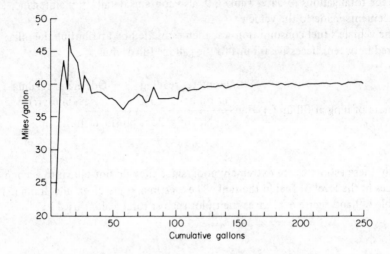

Figure 6.12 Overall estimate of fuel consumption

The CuSum of this data was calculated by setting the standard or reference value at:

$$k = 40 \text{ mpg}$$

The CuSum is

$$S_r = \sum_{i=1}^{r} (M_i - k g_i)$$

where M_i = actual miles covered between ith and $(i+1)$th fill-ups; g_i=No. of gallons filled at ith fill-up.
Thus again $S_1 = (94 - 4 \times 40) = -66$
$\qquad S_2 = -66 + (178 - 3 \times 40) = -8$
$\qquad S_3 = -8 + (163 - 3 \times 40) = +35$
etc.

These 'CuSum' values are given in table 6.9 column (7) and their plot is given in figure 6.12 against total gallons used. The changes which have occurred over the period in fuel consumption are now clearly shown.

Initially the car was only running at 35 mpg and after a total of 54 gallons, it was returned to the garage, where on examination, two burnt out valves were found and car was given a de-coke.

The fuel consumption immediately improved to 44 mpg and then dropped off to about 41 mpg up to a total of 240 gallons when further examinations showed a faulty water pump which was replaced, and the fuel consumption increased again to 45 mpg.

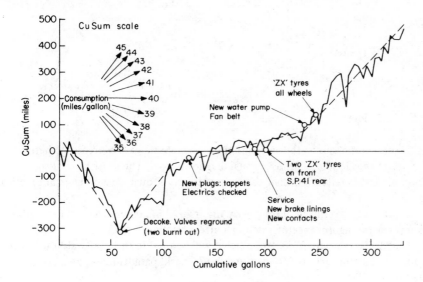

Figure 6.13 CuSum of fuel consumption

This case study shows the power of the CuSum in detecting changes thus enabling the motorist to take corrective action. The fact that the CuSum can successfully detect changes even with such variable data, shows clearly its power as a management diagnostic tool.

This case study resulted in the programme which has developed a CuSum monitor for the private motorist — the Econograph and a computer package for monitoring fuel consumption for large fleet operators.

6.4 Summary

All the examples given have demonstrated the power of the CuSum chart in giving a visual picture of changes in the variable. It has been shown that the CuSum plot is much more sensitive in detecting changes than conventional graphs and thus the CuSum chart is an ideal graph form for visual diagnosis.

Again, it must be stressed that for management decision making to be effective, the apparent changes in the variable must be related to some factor, i.e. diagnosed before taking action.

The use of the CuSum as a 'Management Diagnostic Tool' can be linked to the tests of significance developed in the next chapter. If the visual changes in the variable cannot be 'diagnosed' to a change in practice the significance of this apparent change should be tested before any action is taken.

7. Design of CuSum Control Charts

7.1 Introduction

In the previous chapter, the calculation of the CuSum was covered together with the use of the CuSum chart as a visual diagnostic tool. The sensitivity of the CuSum chart in detecting changes was also clearly shown, with a range of practical examples.

In practice, it is this very sensitivity that makes it advisable wherever possible to test for the significance of any apparent change in the CuSum.

The 'decision interval' control scheme will be used in this book, although other forms of control, such as 'V' mask, parabolic mask, parallel mask, etc., are also used in practice.

7.2 CuSum Control Charts for Variables

Since it is more usually associated with variable control charts, the theory of the application of the CuSum to variables will be covered first.

The CuSum decision taking process is different from that of the Shewhart Charts — CuSum decision taking is based on setting up A.R.L.s (average run length's to detection) at:

(i) Acceptable quality level (A.Q.L.) (which is usually equal to or can be larger than the standard); and

(ii) the reject quality level (R.Q.L.) [†] the level at which detection is required.

Since detection is not required at A.Q.L. the average run length is set arbitrarily at, say, 500, or only a 1 in 500 chance of asserting a change when in fact no change has occurred. This is comparable to Shewhart charts where there is only a 1 in 1000 chance of going outside the action limit when process average is on target. However, different from the Shewhart Charts, a quality level is now chosen at which it is reasonably certain that if the process average changes to this level,

---

[†] The tests given here for detecting a change are one-sided. It should be noted that the test can be used for a change either upwards or downwards.

this change should be detected. This quality level is called the reject quality level (R.Q.L.)

This average run length at R.Q.L. is therefore made small; an A.R.L. of 2 or a 50% chance of detection on any sample and an A.R.L. of 5 or a 20% chance of detection on any sample, are typical of the levels used in practice.

The symbols used in CuSum are given in the list of symbols at the beginning of the book but are also reproduced here.

μ_0 = Acceptable quality level (A.Q.L.)

μ_1 = Reject quality level (R.Q.L.)

k = Reference value

n = Sample size

σ or σ_0 = Process capability

L_0 = Average run length at A.Q.L.(μ_0)

L_1 = Average run length at R.Q.L.(μ_1)

h = Decision interval

The CuSum could be formed with μ_0 as reference value, and a suitable decision rule could be — take action when the current CuSum point rises more than a stated amount (h) over the lowest previous point; this quantity is called the decision interval (h). However, with the decision interval method of control, the reference value k is set at $(\mu_1 + \mu_0)/2$, at a point halfway between the acceptable quality level and the reject quality level. With this value of k, it is only necessary to calculate the decision interval (h) when the CuSum is increasing; when the CuSum is decreasing the value of the decision interval is zero. This procedure will be covered in detail later in the chapter.

The design of variable charts is based on a new Nomogram in table 8* of statistical tables in the Appendix.

The procedure for using this nomogram depends on whether or not the sample size (n) is fixed or not.

(i) Firstly for fixed sample size n:

(a) Define one of the A.R.L.s, that at A.Q.L. say L_0

(b) Calculate $\dfrac{|\mu_1 - k|\sqrt{n}}{\sigma}$

(c) Read off $\dfrac{h\sqrt{n}}{\sigma}$ at intersection of L_0 and $\dfrac{|\mu_1 - k|\sqrt{n}}{\sigma}$

(d) Read off value of L_1 at this intersection point (interpolate if necessary)

(e) Calculate h.

(ii) *Secondly, if sample size is not fixed:*

(a) Define A.R.L.s at both A.Q.L. and R.Q.L.

(b) From nomogram in table 8* where A.R.L.s intercept, read off values of:

$$\frac{|\mu_1 - k|\sqrt{n}}{\sigma} \quad \text{and} \quad \frac{h\sqrt{n}}{\sigma}$$

(c) Calculate sample size (n).
(d) Calculate decision interval (h).

7.2.1 Examples of CuSum Control

No. 1: Sample Size not Fixed

The nominal process average of a manufactured article is 5.0 units and when the process is producing items at this level it should not be interfered with in error more than once in 500 h on average. If, however, the mean rises to 5.2 units, this change should be detected on the average in 5 h. It is known from previous experience that the process is normal with process capability of 0.48 units. Samples are taken once an hour. Calculate the sample size to give this degree of control.

$$L_0 = 500 \quad \mu_0 = 5 \quad \sigma = 0.48$$

Here

$$L_1 = 5.0 \quad \mu_1 = 5.2 \quad k = \frac{\mu_0 + \mu_1}{2} = \frac{5 + 5.2}{2} = 5.1$$

From nomogram in table 8* with $L_0 = 500$, and $L_1 = 5.0$, read off:

$$\frac{|\mu_1 - k|\sqrt{n}}{\sigma} = 0.72$$
$$\frac{h\sqrt{n}}{\sigma} = 3.15$$

at intersection
of $L_0 = 500$ and $L_1 = 5$

Therefore
$$\frac{0.1\sqrt{n}}{0.48} = 0.72$$

Therefore
$$\sqrt{n} = \frac{0.72 \times 0.48}{0.1} = 3.45 \therefore n = 2.45^2 \approx 12$$

Therefore sample size (n) $\doteqdot$ 12.

Also decision interval (h) $= \dfrac{3.15 \times 0.48}{\sqrt{12}} = 0.48$ CuSum units.

Thus control is achieved by plotting the CuSum only wherever the value is increasing and if it returns to zero or below the CuSum plot is terminated. When the Decision Interval exceeds 0.48 there is only a 1 in 500 chance that the process has not changed and the process can now be stated to be out of control. The degree of out of control is of course not available, but there is a 1 in 5 chance of detecting the change in process average from 5.0 to 5.2 units in one sample.

To assist in understanding the effect of varying the reject quality level the CuSum control for a change in the reject quality level to 5.4 is given below.

Here

$$\mu_0 = 5.0 \quad k = 5.2 \quad L_0 = 500$$

$$\mu_1 = 5.4 \quad \sigma = 0.48 \quad L_1 = 5$$

The values of $\dfrac{|\mu_1 - k|\sqrt{n}}{\sigma}$ and $\dfrac{h\sqrt{n}}{\sigma}$ obtained from table 8* remain unchanged.

Therefore

$$\frac{|\mu_1 - k|\sqrt{n}}{\sigma} = 0.72 \text{ and } \frac{h\sqrt{n}}{\sigma} = 3.15$$

or

$$\frac{0.2\sqrt{n}}{0.48} = 0.72 \text{ therefore } \sqrt{n} = 1.7 \text{ and } n = 1.7^2 \approx 3$$

Therefore sample size $(n) \doteq 3$

Thus the sample size can be reduced to 3 to achieve this new level of control with decision interval of:

$$\text{Decision interval } (h) = \frac{3.15 \times 0.48}{\sqrt{3}} = 0.89 \text{ units of CuSum}$$

No. 2: Sample Size Fixed

A sample of size $n = 4$ is taken every hour from a production process. The process produces components to a nominal dimension of 10 mm with process capability $\sigma = 0.02$ mm.

If process average changes to 10.02 mm, the control should detect the change. Discuss the control which can be achieved.

Here $\mu = 10.00 \quad \sigma = 0.02 \quad \mu_1 = 10.02 \quad k = 10.01 \quad n = 4$
Let $L_0 = 500$; the question is what is the value of L_1?

$$\frac{|\mu_1 - k|\sqrt{n}}{\sigma} = \frac{0.01 \times \sqrt{4}}{0.02} = 1.00$$

From table 8*, the intersection of $\dfrac{|\mu_1 - k|\sqrt{n}}{\sigma} = 1$ and $L_0 = 500$

gives $L_1 = 3$ and $\dfrac{h\sqrt{n}}{\sigma} = 2.3$

Therefore decision interval $(h) = \dfrac{2.3 \times 0.02}{\sqrt{4}} = 0.23$ units of CuSum

Thus this scheme will detect a change in process average to 10.02 mm in three samples on the average.

Consider now, what will be the A.R.L. to detect a change to 10.01 mm? Here $\mu_1 = 10.01$ $\mu_0 = 10.00$ therefore $k = 10.005$

Therefore

$$\frac{|\mu_1 - k|\sqrt{n}}{\sigma} = \frac{0.005 \times \sqrt{4}}{0.02} = 0.5$$

From nomogram (table 8*), at intersection of

$$\frac{|\mu_1 - k|\sqrt{n}}{\sigma} = 0.5 \text{ and } L_0 = 500,$$

gives $L_1 = 10$, or it will require 10 samples on the average to detect a change in process average to 10.01.

It is interesting here to compare the sensitivity of this CuSum scheme with the Shewhart chart. For CuSum scheme with

     A.Q.L. = 10.00 mm $L_0 = 500$ R.Q.L. = 10.01 mm $L_1 = 10$
     $\sigma = 0.02$ and $n = 4$

Thus if, as shown, process average changes to 10.01 mm, the average run length for detection is 10 with CuSum control.

The comparable Shewhart chart is:

Warning limit = $10 \pm 0.98 \times 0.02 = 10 \pm 01.96$ mm = 10 ± 0.02 mm
Action limit = $10 \pm 1.545 \times 0.02 = 10 \pm 0.309$ mm = 10 ± 0.03 mm
from table 4*.

Thus if process average changes to 10.01 mm, the probability of a sample average falling outside the *action limit* is given by

Upper
limit $U = \dfrac{10.03 - 10.01}{\dfrac{\sigma}{\sqrt{n}}} = \dfrac{0.02}{0.01} = 2$

Lower
limit $U = \dfrac{9.7 - 10.01}{0.01} = 4.0$

(negligible) (see figure 7.1)

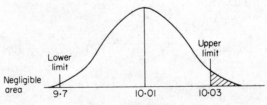

Figure 7.1

Therefore probability of falling outside action limit = 0.02275 from table *2

Therefore average run length to detection = $\dfrac{1}{0.02275} \doteq 44$

Thus the Shewhart chart would require 44 samples on average to detect this change, or over 4 times as long as the CuSum. The comparison of the schemes will be more fully covered in Chapter 8.

No. 3: Using the Decision Interval to Detect out of Control

To fully illustrate the plotting of a CuSum chart and the use of the decision interval (h), 15 samples of size $n = 4$ were simulated for a normal distribution with mean $\mu_0 = 0$ and standard deviation $\sigma = 2.0$. The process mean was then changed to 1.0 and a further 15 samples of size $n = 4$ taken. The results are shown in table 7.1.

Design of CuSum Here $\mu_0 = 0.00$ $\sigma = 2.0$ $\mu_1 = 1.00$ $k = 0.5$ $n = 4$
Let average run length to detection at μ_0 be 500, i.e. $L_0 = 500$
Also

$$\frac{|\mu_1 - k|\sqrt{n}}{\sigma} = \frac{0.5 \times \sqrt{4}}{2} = 0.5$$

From nomogram table 8* at intersection $L_0 = 500$ and $\dfrac{|\mu_1 - k|\sqrt{n}}{\sigma} = 0.5$

This gives

$$\frac{h\sqrt{n}}{\sigma} = 4.4 \quad \text{and} \quad L_1 = 10$$

Therefore decision interval $(h) = \dfrac{4.4 \times 2.0}{\sqrt{4}} = 4.4$ units of CuSum and average

run length to detection at process average of 1.0 is 10.

In practice it is only necessary to calculate the decision interval (h) when the CuSum plot is increasing. When the CuSum is decreasing the implicit value of (h) is zero.

Both the CuSum and the decision interval values are shown in table 7.1, and the decision interval chart is shown plotted in figure 7.2. While most textbooks advocate the plotting of the values of h, the plot being called a modified CuSum chart, there is, in the author's opinion, little to justify this in that the plot gives no additional information. However, wherever possible, the CuSum should be plotted as this gives a much fuller understanding of the process and its changes. Figure 7.3 shows this CuSum plot and the detection of the change.

Thus, in practice, it is not necessary to plot the CuSum chart when using the decision interval method to detect a change, but the plotting of the chart will give a fuller understanding of the process.

Table 7.1 Sample average ($n = 4$ $\sigma = 2.0$) ($\mu = 0$ for 1st 15 samples. $\mu = 1$ for 2nd 15 samples)

Sample No. (mean $\mu=0$ $\sigma=2.0$)	1	2	3	4	5	6	7	8
Sample average $\bar{X}_i$	-1.04	0.09	0.32	-1.28	1.10	-1.31	1.15	-0.07
CuSum $\Sigma(\bar{X}_i-0.5)$	-1.54	-1.95	-2.13	-3.91	-3.31	-5.12	-4.47	-5.04
Decision int. (h)	0	0	0	0	+0.60	0	0.65	0.08

Sample No. (mean $\mu=0$ $\sigma=2.0$)	9	10	11	12	13	14	15
Sample average $\bar{X}_i$	0.67	1.00	0.31	-1.27	-0.05	-0.72	-2.12
CuSum $\Sigma(\bar{X}_i-0.5)$	-4.87	-4.37	-4.56	-6.33	-6.88	-8.10	-10.72
Decision int. (h)	0.25	0.75	0.56	0	0	0	0

Sample No. (mean $\mu=1.0$ $\sigma=2.0$)	16	17	18	19	20	21	22	23
Sample average $\bar{X}_i$	1.39	0.20	1.57	-1.00	2.70	0.32	1.84	0.52
CuSum $\Sigma(\bar{X}_i-0.5)$	-9.83	-10.13	-9.06	-10.56	-8.36	-8.54	-7.20	-7.18
Decision int. (h)	0.89	0.59	1.66	0.16	2.36	2.18	3.52	3.54

Sample No. (mean $\mu=1.0$ $\sigma=2.0$)	24	25	26	27	28	29	30
Sample average $\bar{X}_i$	0.42	1.56	1.13	1.56	0.98	1.49	-1.29
CuSum $\Sigma(\bar{X}_i-0.5)$	-7.26	-6.20	-5.57	-4.51	-4.03	-3.04	-4.83
Decision int. (h)	3.46	4.52†	5.05	6.11	6.59	7.58	5.79

† Significant increase of mean is indicated at this sample or with an actual run length of 10 samples − coincidence that run length detained on this trial was the same as the average run length (L_r).

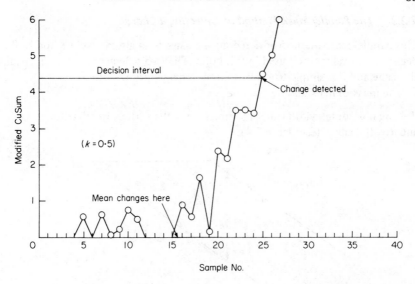

Figure 7.2 Modified CuSum chart (decision interval control)

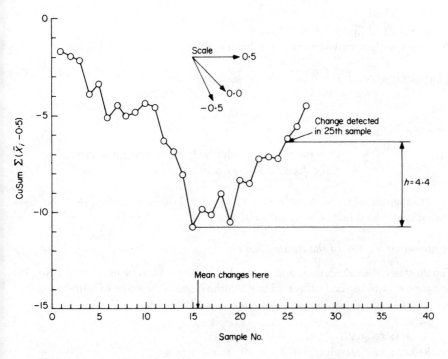

Figure 7.3 CuSum chart. Decision interval scheme for controlling the increase of the mean

7.2.2   The Parallel Mask Method of Detecting a Change

This parallel mask method of detecting a change is an alternative method to the decision interval method used in this book. The two schemes are mathematically the same and it is simple to convert either scheme into the other.

The mask dimensions are:

d = the horizontal width (no. of samples), b = the vertical width (CuSum Units) and θ = the angle (see figure 7.4).

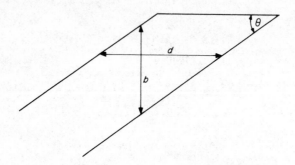

Figure 7.4 Parallel mask

Referring to figure 7.4, $b = d \tan \theta$
The relationships between the two schemes are:

Horizontal width $d = \dfrac{h}{(k-\mu_0)}$ (No. of samples)

and

Vertical width $b = h$ (CuSum units)

where $k = \dfrac{(\mu_0 + \mu_1)}{2}$ is the reference value and, h is the decision interval for the decision interval scheme.

Thus, given values of the reference value (k) and decision interval (h) it is simple to calculate the dimensions of a Parallel Mask.

Example of the Use of the Parallel Mask

To illustrate the calculations and use of the parallel mask scheme, example No. 3 on page 81 will be used, thus enabling a comparison to be made of both methods of control, namely the decision interval and parallel mask.

Here

Acceptable quality level $\mu_0 = 0$ $L_0 = 500$

Reject quality level $\mu_1 = 1$ $L_1 = 10$ $\sigma = 2$ $n = 4$

For decision interval control (see page 81)

Decision interval $h = 4.4$
Reference value $k = 0.5$
The mask dimensions are therefore,

Horizontal width $d = \dfrac{h}{(k-\mu_0)} = \dfrac{4.4}{0.5} = 8.8$ (units = No. of samples)

Vertical width $b = d \times (k-\mu_0) = 8.8 \times 0.5 = 4.4$ (CuSum units)

N.B. When using the parallel mask (and also the 'V' mask, a similar scheme) to detect changes, its design is based on the CuSum being calculated as:

$$\sum_{i=1}^{n} (X_i - \mu_0) \text{ and}$$

not $\displaystyle\sum_{i=1}^{n} (X_i - k)$ as used in the decision interval scheme.

This change of base can be confusing and although the schemes are basically similar and the interrelationships between them are simple, in practice only one type of scheme should be used in order to eliminate any confusion.

The CuSum is shown in figure 7.5. The method of detecting the change is to place the leading edge of the mask on the latest CuSum plot and if any point on

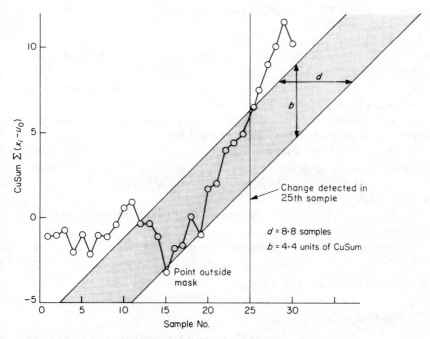

Figure 7.5 Parallel mask for detecting change

the CuSum plot is outside the mask, e.g. its trailing edge, then there has been a change; in figure 7.5 the change is detected at sample No. 25.

When using this mask technique to detect changes as with any CuSum plot, the choice of the scales of the axes is important as far as visual interpretation is concerned.

In practice, it has been found that the scales should be chosen to give an angle of 45°, e.g. $\theta = 45°$ for the mask — angles greater than 60° give charts relatively insensitive to changes. Again angles below 30° tend to accentuate the random fluctuations in the data.

7.2.3   Comparison of the Decision Interval Method and the Parallel Mask Method of Detecting a Change

The two schemes are compared here. Before going on to the comparison it must be stressed again that both schemes are mathematically equivalent and the differences are in method and operation rather than basic theory.

In the author's opinion, decision interval schemes are generally preferable to parallel mask schemes, for the following reasons:

(1) The decision interval scheme requires less chart plotting — as the decision interval (h) is measured from the past lowest cumulative sum obtained; for a one-sided test, the modified cumulative sum chart has a lower boundary zero and upper boundary (h) (see figure 7.2). Because of this, the modified decision interval chart requires less plotting.

(2) The cumulative sum in modified decision interval charts does not run off the paper since the ordinate of all points except the one giving the signal is confined between zero and h.

(3) The plotting in the decision interval scheme may be dispensed with altogether — the charting principle involved can be easily applied to a table of successive results. In this table, the values of the cumulative sum are simply checked against the pre-determined decision interval (h) (see table 7.1).

(4) The modified decision interval scheme by table is more accurate since it is operated on the basis of manipulating figures. On the other hand, the decision by the parallel mask schemes depends largely on the accuracy of plotting and a certain degree of subjective judgement when using the mask.

(5) The decision interval scheme does not need a mask, hence its operation may be simpler.

(6) The scale of the decision interval chart is relatively unimportant.

7.3   Attribute CuSum Control Systems

7.3.1   Introduction

The design of attribute CuSum control charts is based on the same concepts to those used in variable control charts (see previous Section 7.2). The design parameters are:

The acceptable quality level = p_1

The reject quality level = p_2

Sample size = n

Average run length to detection at A.Q.L. = L_0 (L_0 = 500 in this book)

Average run length to detection at R.Q.L. = L_1

Table 9* gives the data for the design of attribute CuSum control schemes, computed using the Poisson distribution as an approximation to the Binomial distribution, with

Average No. of defects/sample at A.Q.L. (m_1) = np_1

Average No. of defects/sample at R.Q.L. (m_2) = np_2

*Notes on table 9**

Since the decision interval (h) and the reference value (k) can only take integral values, the values of m_1 tabulated are of necessity discrete. A selection of feasible schemes is included in table 9, chosen to give a range of values of m_1 up to 10.

The table gives values of m_2 and R where $R = m_1/m_2$ for range of values of L_1, the average run length to detection at R.Q.L. Where alternative schemes were available, the scheme giving the lower value of R for a given value of L_1 was chosen.

Design of CuSum Control Schemes

As with variable charts, the design procedure depends on whether or not the sample size (n) is fixed or not.

1. Schemes with given sample size n

  (a) Calculate $m_1 = np_1$

  (b) From table 9*, for nearest value of m_1 read off the values of m_2 for various values of L_1; also read off

  Decision interval (h)

  Reference value (k)

2. Schemes where the sample size is not fixed

  (a) Define A.R.L. (L_1) and R.Q.L. (p_2)

  (b) Calculate $R = \dfrac{m_2}{m_1} = \dfrac{np_2}{np_1} = \dfrac{p_2}{p_1}$

  (c) From table 9* read off scheme which gives required value of R at design value of L_1. If value of R cannot be found in table 9*, scheme is not feasible, and either the R.Q.L. or L_1 must be changed.

  (d) With new value of either R.Q.L. and/or L_1 repeat steps (b) and (c).

7.3.2 Examples on Design of Attribute Control Scheme

No. 1: Fixed Sample Size

Samples of size $n = 100$ are taken every hour from a mass production process. Given that the acceptable quality level of the process is 2%, set up a CuSum control system to detect changes in the process.

Acceptable quality level $p_1 = 0.02$; sample size $(n) = 100$

Average defects/sample at A.Q.L. $m_1 = np_1 = 100 \times 0.02 = 2.0$

Table 9* with $m_1 = 2.00$ and $L_0 = 500$, gives the nearest scheme as

$$\left. \begin{array}{l} \text{Decision interval } (h) = 6 \\ \text{Reference value } (k) = 3 \end{array} \right\} \text{with } m_1 = 1.96$$

The sensitivity of the scheme to detecting changes in process average is also given in table 9*.

With $m_1 = 1.96$ $m_2 = 7.11$ for $L_1 = 2$, $m_2 = 4.74$ for $L_1 = 4$, etc.

or a change in process quality level to 7.11% will be detected in 2 samples on the average; again a change to 4.74% will be detected in 4 samples on the average, etc. Table 7.2 summarises this sensitivity.

It is interesting to compare the sensitivity of CuSum schemes at detecting changes with similar Shewhart schemes.

In the case of the Shewhart scheme with similar A.R.L. at p_1, namely 500, then the *'action'* limit for asserting a change will run only a 1 in 500 risk of having a sample outside its limit when process is running at or below its acceptable quality level.

Here $m_1 = np_1 = 100 \times 0.02 = 2.00$

From table 1*, *action limit* for risk of 1/500 is 6.5, actually a 0.0011 risk of exceeding 6 defects (closest to 0.002).

The average number of samples in the Shewhart system to detect changes given in table 7.2 are given in table 7.3.

Table 7.2 CuSum control sensitivity

Process average changes to (%)	Average No. of samples to detection (L_1)
7.1	2
4.74	4
4.3	5
4.15	6
3.7	8
3.6	9
3.5	10

Table 7.3 Shewhart scheme sensitivity

Process average changes to (%)	Average No. of samples to detection (L_1)
7.1	1.8
4.7	5.1
4.3	6.9
4.10	8.2
3.79	12.2
3.6	13.6
3.5	15.3

Comparing tables 7.2 and 7.3 shows that the sensitivity of the CuSum is greater than the similar Shewhart scheme — apart from the change from 2.00 to 7.11% — a major change — when the schemes are alike and in fact the Shewhart has a slight advantage. This comparison of the CuSum and Shewhart schemes will be covered more fully in the next chapter.

No. 2: Fixed Sample Size

Every month a sample of 200 completed forms selected randomly are checked for errors. The office manager wished to maintain a standard of 2% errors.

Set up CuSum control and discuss its sensitivity.

Here $p_1 = 0.02$ $n = 200$ $L_0 = 500$
therefore $m_1 = np = 200 \times 0.02 = 4.00$
Refer to table 9*, with $m_1 = 4.16$ (closest value to $m_1 = 4$). For $m_1 = 4.16$ CuSum scheme is
Decision interval $h = 7$
Reference value $k = 6$
The table also enables the sensitivity of the scheme to be calculated. Thus this scheme will detect a change in process average to $7.50/200 \times 100\%$ or 3.75% in 5 samples on the average.

No. 3. Fixed Sample Size

This example illustrates the complete procedure for setting up control. Samples of 200 taken every hour from a production process gave the number of defects shown in table 7.4.

Table 7.4

Sample No.	Number of defects									
	1	2	3	4	5	6	7	8	9	10
1 – 10	1	0	2	3	1	0	0	2	1	0
11 – 20	0	1	1	0	5	2	1	0	0	1
21 – 25	0	3	2	1	0					

Average defects/sample = 1.1.

Set Up CuSum Control. The first step is to check whether process is in control. The actual distribution compared with the Poisson is given in table 7.5.

The χ^2 test shows no significant difference. Thus there is no evidence that the process is out of control.

The A.Q.L. will be taken as the current process average in this example. Thus

A.Q.L. $= \dfrac{1.1}{200} \times 100\%$ or 0.55%

Table 7.5

No. of defects/sample	0	1	2	3	4	5	Total
Actual distribution	10	8	4	2	0	1	25
				7			
Poisson distribution†	8.3	9.5	5	1.8	0.5	0.1	25.2
				7.4			

† From table 2* with $m = 1.1$

From table 9* with $m_1 = 1.1$, closest reading is $m_1 = 1.05$, giving: Decision interval $(h) = 4$

Reference value $(k) = 2$

Reference to table 9* also shows that this CuSum control scheme will detect a change to 1.41% in process average in 5 samples on the average.

No.4: Sample Size Not Fixed

Here if the R.Q.L. is fixed, then the sample size can be determined to give this degree of control.

Consider the previous example.

Here process average = 0.0055 or 0.55% defective

Control is required to detect a change in process average to 0.90% or higher; what is the sample size required for this control?

Thus Reject quality level (R.Q.L.) $p_2 = 0.0090$

Acceptable quality level (A.Q.L.) $p_1 = 0.0055$

Let n = the sample size required, then $R = \dfrac{0.0090}{0.0055} \doteqdot 1.64$

Let $L_1 = 4$, then from table 9*, gives for R, 1.6 nearest value.

$m_1 = 9.00$ and $m_2 = 14.59$
$h = 12$ and $k = 11$

Thus sample size $n = \dfrac{9.00}{0.0055} = 1636 \doteqdot 1650$

and actual R.Q.L. $= \dfrac{m_2}{n} = \dfrac{14.59}{1650} = 0.0088$

or 0.88% defective.

Consider now the effect of easing the control to a reject quality level of 1.5% with $L_1 = 4$. Here $R = \dfrac{0.015}{0.0055} = 2.73$

For $L_1 = 4$ table 9* gives $R = 2.75$ (nearest value).

Decision interval $(h) = 4$

Reference value $(k) = 3$

and $m_1 = 1.52$

Therefore sample size $n = \dfrac{1.52}{0.0055} = 276.4 \doteq 300$

7.4 Problems for Solution

(1) Samples of size 9 are taken every half-hour from a production process. The process produces to a nominal dimension of 20 mm with process capability of 0.02 mm.

If the process average changes to 20.02 mm, the control procedure should detect the change.

Design a CuSum control procedure for controlling the process.

(2) Design the CuSum control system for a process given the following data:

Process average $= 100$ mm
Process capability $= 1$mm
Reject quality level $= 101$ mm
A.R.L. at acceptable quality level $= 500$
A.R.L. at reject quality level $= 5$

(3) (a) In the growing of cotton, if more than 1 plant in 20 is infested, then the crop should be sprayed with insecticide.

Given that infection is randomly distributed and samples are taken every week, calculate the sample size (n) and set up the CuSum chart to determine when to spray, such that if the level of infestation is 6% this infestation level will be detected in 2 samples on the average.

The standard level of infestation is 2%, at which level spraying should not occur.

(b) With the control scheme developed in (a), given the following number of infested plants in the samples, does the CuSum scheme detect the change?

Sample No.	1	2	3	4	5	6	7	8	9	10
No. of infested plants	5	3	2	4	5	5	9	3	2	4

(c) If sample size (n) is increased to 200, show how the control scheme can be tightened.

(4) In measuring a vehicle's fuel consumption, the following procedure is used.

Four gallons of petrol are put into the tank, whenever the vehicle's red indicator light indicating low fuel level in the tank comes on.

Given that the standard deviation of miles covered on a gallon $= 2.0$, i.e. variation due to differences in the level of fuel in the tank at fill up, in driving conditions, etc., set up a CuSum control to enable motorists to detect changes in fuel consumption.

The standard miles/gallon is 35 for the vehicle.

(5) The following data gives the overheads of a company over the last 6 periods.

Given that the target overheads/period is £10 000 with a standard deviation of £500.

Set up CuSum control.

Period	Overheads
1	£ 9 780
2	£10 700
3	£10 900
4	£11 200
5	£11 000
6	£10 400

Does the data given show any evidence of out of control?

(6) Table 7.6 shows the number of accidents per month at a manufacturing company. Analyse the data and set up CuSum control.

Table 7.6 No. of accidents

	1971	1972	1973	1974
January	3	4	4	5
February	2	2	3	
March	5	2	1	
April	2	1	8	
May	3	2	3	
June	6	5	4	
July	0	0	3	
August	4	2	4	
September	2	4	4	
October	3	5	2	
November	1	4	3	
December	4	2	3	

(7) Data from a production shop over the last 20 weeks gave the following weekly figures for the average bonus earned.

Wk. 1 102	Wk. 6 103	Wk. 11 104	Wk. 16 104
Wk. 2 108	Wk. 7 104	Wk. 12 105	Wk. 17 104
Wk. 3 98	Wk. 8 100	Wk. 13 102	Wk. 18 102
Wk. 4 104	Wk. 9 105	Wk. 14 107	Wk. 19 105
Wk. 5 102	Wk. 10 106	Wk. 15 101	Wk. 20 102

Analyse and set up CuSum control.

7.5 Solutions to Problems

No. 1

Here $n = 9, \mu_0 = 20$ mm, $\sigma = 0.02$ mm, $\mu_1 = 20.02$ mm

Then $k = \dfrac{\mu_0 + \mu_1}{2} = 20.01$ mm

and $\dfrac{|\mu_1 - k|\sqrt{n}}{\sigma} = \dfrac{0.01 \times \sqrt{9}}{0.02} = 1.5$

Let $L_0 = 500$. Table 8* at the intersection of $\dfrac{|\mu_1 - k|\sqrt{n}}{\sigma} = 1.5$ and

$L_0 = 500$ gives $\dfrac{h\sqrt{n}}{\sigma} = 1.5$ and $L_1 \doteqdot 1.7$ (by interpolation)

Therefore decision interval $(h) = \dfrac{1.5 \times 0.02}{\sqrt{9}} = 0.01$

Doubling the sample size (n) to 18 will enable even tighter control to be achieved. Since L_1 is already low, namely $L_1 = 1.7$, there is little point in keeping R.Q.L. at 20.02 mm — detection can be obtained at a lower value.

Here $n = 18, \sigma = 0.02, L_0 = 500, \mu_0 = 20$ mm, $\mu_1 = ?$
  Let A.R.L. $L_1 = 3$, what is R.Q.L. for the scheme?
  At intersection of $L_0 = 500$ and $L_1 = 3$ in table 8*,
  $\dfrac{h\sqrt{n}}{\sigma} = 2.3$ and $\dfrac{|\mu_1 - k|\sqrt{n}}{\sigma} = 1.0$
  Therefore decision interval $(h) = 0.01$ mm.
  Also $|\mu_1 - k| = \dfrac{1.0 \times 0.02}{\sqrt{18}} = 0.0047$
  Therefore R.Q.L. $= 20 + 2 \times 0.0047 = 20.0084$ mm $\doteqdot 20.01$ mm

No. 2

Given $L_0 = 500$ $\sigma = 1.00$ $L_1 = 5$ $\mu_0 = 100$ $\mu_1 = 101$
Therefore $k = 100.5$
Therefore from table 8*, at intersection of $L_0 = 500$ and $L = 5$

$\dfrac{|\mu_1 - k|\sqrt{n}}{\sigma} = 0.75$

and $\dfrac{h\sqrt{n}}{\sigma} = 3.15$

Therefore $\dfrac{0.5\sqrt{n}}{1.00} = 0.75$

Therefore $\sqrt{n} \doteq 1.5$

Sample size $(n) \doteq 3$

Also

$$\dfrac{h\sqrt{3}}{1.00} = 3.15$$

Therefore decision interval $(h) = \dfrac{3.15 \times 1.00}{\sqrt{3}} = 1.82$ units of CuSum

No. 3

Here

$p_1 = 0.02$
$L_1 = 2$ $R = \dfrac{p_2}{p_1} = \dfrac{0.06}{0.02} = 3.0$
$p_2 = 0.06$
Let $L_0 = 500$

From table 9*, for value $R = 3.1$ at $L_1 = 2, m_1 = 2.6$.

Therefore the sample size $n = \dfrac{2.60}{0.02} = 130$

CuSum scheme is:
    Reference value $k = 4$
    Decision interval $h = 6$

Table 7.7 gives the calculation of the Decision Interval.

Table 7.7

Sample No.	1	2	3	4	5	6	7	8	9	10
No. of infected plants (x_i)	5	3	2	4	5	5	9	3	2	4
CuSum $\Sigma\,(x_i - 4)$	+1	0	-2	-2	-1	0	+5	+4	+4	+4
Decision interval (h)	+1	0	0	0	+1	+2	+7*			

Therefore change detected at Sample No. 7.

Sample size n increased to 200

Here clearly the scheme will be more sensitive in detecting changes.

$$m_1 = np_1 = 200 \times 0.02 = 4.0$$

From table 9* with $m_1 = 3.89$ (closest to 4.0), $m_2 = 10.28$ for $L_1 = 2$, $m_2 = 7.24$ for $L_1 = 5$ etc.

The scheme will now detect a change to 5.14% infestation with an average run length (A.R.L.) of 2, or a change to 3.62% with an average run length of 5.

No. 4

Standard miles/gallons $\mu_0 = 35$
Standard deviation $\sigma = 2.00$
No. of gallons/fill up $n = 4$
Let $L_0 = 500$ and $L_1 = 3$. Here detection of a drop in fuel consumption will be demonstrated. Clearly, a similar control can be calculated for detecting improvement.

From table 8*, at intersection of $L_0 = 500$ and $L_1 = 3$

$$\frac{|\mu_1 - k|\sqrt{n}}{\sigma} = 1.00$$

and
$$\frac{h\sqrt{n}}{\sigma} = 2.3$$

Therefore $|\mu_1 - k| = 1.00 \times \dfrac{2.00}{\sqrt{4}} = 1.00$

Therefore $\mu_1 = 33$ mpg

Decision interval $(h) = \dfrac{2.3 \times 2}{\sqrt{4}} = 2.3$ units of CuSum

Thus the CuSum control will detect a drop in fuel consumption from 35 mpg to 33 mpg in three fill ups on the average.

No. 5

Here $\mu = £10\ 000$
$\sigma = £500$
$n = 1$
Let $L_0 = 500$ and $L_1 = 5$. From table 8*, at intersection of $L_0 = 500$ and $L_1 = 5$

$$\frac{|\mu_1 - k|\sqrt{n}}{\sigma} = 0.72$$

and
$$\frac{h\sqrt{n}}{\sigma} = 3.2$$

Therefore $|\mu_1 - k| = \dfrac{0.72 \times 500}{\sqrt{1}} = 360$

Table 7.8

Period	1	2	3	4	5	6
Overheads (x_i)	£9 780	£10 700	£10 900	£ 11 200	£11 000	£10 400
CuSum $\Sigma(x_i-10\,400)$	£−580	£− 240	£ + 300	£+ 1140		
Decision int. (h)	—	£ + 340	£ + 880	£ + 1720†		

†Change detected in 4th period.

Table 7.9

No. of accidents	0	1	2	3	4	5	6	7	8	Total
Frequency	2	3	9	8	9	4	1	0	1	37
Poisson probability	0.05	0.14	0.22	0.22	0.17	0.11	0.06	0.03	0.01	1.01
Poisson frequency	1.8	5.2	8.1	8.1	6.3	3.7	2.2	1.1	0.4	36.9

(Frequency: 0 and 1 grouped as 5; 6, 7 and 8 grouped as 6. Poisson frequency: 0 and 1 grouped as 7; 5, 6, 7 and 8 grouped as 7.4.)

giving $\mu = £10\ 720$
and reference value $k = £10\ 360$

Also decision interval $h = \dfrac{3.2 \times 500}{1} = 1600$ CuSum Units

Table 7.8 gives the decision interval values.

No. 6

To test hypothesis that process is in control, compile table 7.9.

Average number of accidents/month $m = 3.1$ per month'.

$$\chi^2 = \frac{(7-5)^2}{7} + \frac{(9-8.1)^2}{8.1} + \frac{(8-8.1)^2}{8.1} + \frac{(9-6.3)^2}{6.3} + \frac{(6-7.4)^2}{7.4}$$

$$\doteqdot 2.1$$

Referring to table 3*, $\chi^2_{0.05} = 11.07$
Thus data shows no evidence of out of control.

CuSum Control

From table 9*
   Decision interval $h = 6$
   Reference value $k = 5$ with $m_1 = 3.24$ (closest value to $m_1 = 3.1$)

The sensitivity is also available from table 9*. Since the reference value $k = 5$ is higher than all the accident readings (except April 1973), there is little point in computing the decision interval.

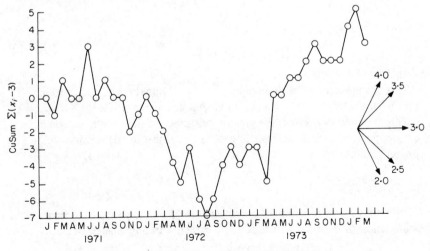

Figure 7.6 CuSum chart. Number of accidents (reference value $k = 3$)

However figure 7.6 shows the CuSum chart (reference value $k = 3$) and visually there appears to have been a change in accident rate at around the 20th month, or August, 1972. However, unless any 'a priori' reason can be given for this change, no action should be taken until further data is available.

Assume that an 'a priori' reason can be given for the change, then the change can be shown to be significant by comparing the change in *averages* before and after.

Dividing the data around this period gives:

Accident rate = 2.65/month up to August, 1972.

Accident rate = 3.5/month after August, 1972

or an apparent increase in the accident rate.

The following approximate test can be used:

Let m_1 = Accident rate/month before change

       m_2 = Accident rate/month after change

       n_1 = No. of months data before change

       n_2 = No. of months data after change.

Null Hypothesis That no change has occurred. Therefore the best estimate of the accident is

$$\text{Rate over period } m = \frac{m_1 \times m + m_1 \times n_2}{n_1 + n_2}$$

$$\text{Therefore } U = \frac{(n_1 m_1 - n_2 m_2) - m(n_1 - n_2)}{[(n_1 + n_2)m]^{1/2}}$$

Here $m_1 = 2.65 \; m_2 = 3.5 \; n_1 = 20 \; n_2 = 17$

$$m = \frac{53 + 62}{20 + 17} = 3.1$$

$$\text{Therefore } U = \frac{(53 - 67 - 3.1\,(20 - 17))}{\sqrt{115}} = \frac{23.3}{10.7} = -2.17$$

or significant at 5% level.

This change can just be detected by this approximate test, but, only if 'a priori' knowledge gives a reason for change at August, 1972.

This example shows how the greater sensitivity of the CuSum can be linked to more powerful statistical tests in order to establish the significance of an apparent change.

No. 7

Assume that bonus rate has remained constant over the period — a visual examination of the time series shows no evidence of any change.

$$\text{Then Standard deviation } \sigma = \left[\frac{\Sigma(x_1 - \bar{x})^2}{20 - 1} \right]^{\frac{1}{2}} = 2.00$$

and   Average bonus earned $\bar{x} = \dfrac{\Sigma x_i}{20} \doteq 103.3$

Let $\mu_0 = 103.3$, the present average

and $L_0 = 200$ (a relatively low value, since the penalty for being wrong is not severe).

$\quad L_1 = 3$

Then from table 8*, at intersection of $L_0 = 200$ and $L_1 = 3$,

$$\dfrac{(\mu_1 - k)\sqrt{n}}{\sigma} = 0.92$$

and $\quad \dfrac{h\sqrt{n}}{\sigma} = 2.10$

Thus $(\mu_1 - k) = \dfrac{0.92 \times 2.00}{\sqrt{1}} = 1.84$

or $\mu_1 = 103.3 + 2 \times 1.84 = 107$

and reference value $(k) = 105.1 \simeq 105$

Decision interval $(h) = \dfrac{2.10 \times 2.0}{\sqrt{1}} = 4.20$ units of CuSum

Thus the scheme will detect an increase in average bonus earnings to 107 in 3 weeks, on the average.

8. Comparison of the British Standard (Shewhart) and CuSum Control Systems

8.1 Introduction

The British Standard (Shewhart) control system, described in Chapter 5 and the CuSum control system, described in Chapter 7 are compared in this chapter.

The basis of the comparison is their efficiency in detecting changes in the process average, measured by the average run length to detection, or the expected number of samples required to detect this change. With the research which is continuing into the distribution of the run lengths to detection, it is suggested that, in future, the 95% percentile could also be used, i.e. the run length that only has a 5% chance of being exceeded.

In order to ensure a fair comparison between the CuSum and Shewhart control schemes, it is necessary to make their respective average run lengths to detection (L_0) the same when the process is running at the acceptable quality level.

Comparisons given where detection is defined as a point outside the *action limit* of $\pm 3.09 \, \sigma / \sqrt{n}$ in Shewhart schemes are not fair since the CuSum is basically a one-sided test, and the average run length to detection of the CuSum would also have to be 1000. Since the maximum design value used in this book of L_0 is 500, comparisons which make no adjustment to the Shewhart limits are biased in favour of the CuSum scheme.

Here the average run length to detection, on the basis of a one-sided test, has been taken as $L_0 = 500$ for both schemes. In the case of the Shewhart variable schemes, this has the effect of setting the limits for detection at $\pm 2.88 \, \sigma / \sqrt{n}$ compared with their normal design value of $\pm 3.09 \, \sigma / \sqrt{n}$.

8.2 Variable Control – Comparison of CuSum and Shewhart Schemes

As stated, in order to give a fair comparison between the schemes, detection has to be redefined for the Shewhart scheme, such that the average run length to detection is 500, at the acceptable quality level, based on a one-sided test.

From table 2*, the one-sided limits are thus $+ 2.88 \, \sigma / \sqrt{n}$ and $- 2.88 \, \sigma / \sqrt{n}$ or if in the detection of an increase in the process average, the detection limit is set at $+ 2.88 \, \sigma / \sqrt{n}$ above the acceptable process average, then there is only a

100

1 in 500 chance of asserting that the process is out of control when it is operating at its Acceptable Quality Level or an A.R.L. (L_0) of 500.

The following example illustrates the calculations used in the comparison.

Process capability (σ) = 1.5
Sample size (n) = 9
Process standard (μ_0) = 10

What is the A.R.L. for detecting a change in the process average to 10.9?

Calculation of ARL for Shewhart Scheme

Deviation from process average = 0.9

Standard deviation of sample averages $\left(\dfrac{\sigma}{\sqrt{n}}\right) = \dfrac{1.5}{\sqrt{9}} = 0.5$

Therefore deviation from process average (in multiples of $\sigma/\sqrt{n}$) $= \dfrac{0.9}{0.5} = 1.8$
(see figure 8.1)

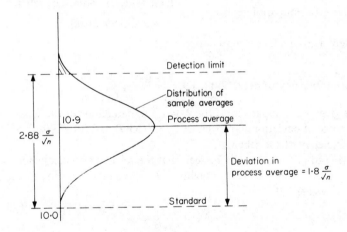

Figure 8.1

Probability of a point falling outside limit when process average = 10.9 is obtained by

$$U = \dfrac{2.88 \ \dfrac{\sigma}{\sqrt{n}} - 1.8 \ \dfrac{\sigma}{\sqrt{n}}}{\dfrac{\sigma}{\sqrt{n}}} = 1.08$$

From table 2*, probability of point outside limit = 0.1379
Therefore A.R.L. to detection for Shewhart = 1/0.1379 = 7.3 samples

Calculation of A.R.L. for CuSum Scheme

Here $\mu_0 = 10.00$ $\sigma = 1.5$ $L_0 = 500$
   $\mu_1 = 10.90$ $n = 9$
Therefore $k = 10.45$
Also $\dfrac{|\mu_1 - k|\sqrt{n}}{\sigma} = \dfrac{0.45 \times \sqrt{9}}{1.5} = 0.90$
From nomogram in table 8*, at intersection $L_0 = 500$
and $\dfrac{|\mu_1 - k|\sqrt{n}}{\sigma} = 0.90$
$L_1 = 3.75$ (interpolating on chart), or average run length to detection = 3.75

The two schemes will be compared in their relative speeds of detecting changes in the process average.

The comparison measure proposed is:

Relative efficiency of detection $(\epsilon) = \dfrac{\text{Time taken by Shewhart scheme}}{\text{Time taken by CuSum scheme}}$

to detect a given change in process average.
Therefore

Relative efficiency of detection $(\epsilon) = \dfrac{\text{A.R.L. of Shewhart}}{\text{A.R.L. of CuSum}}$

Table 8.1 gives the comparison of the A.R.L.s to detection for the schemes over the range of deviation in process average from 0 to 2.88 $\sigma/\sqrt{n}$ together with relative efficiency of the schemes.

Referring to table 8.1, it will be seen that the relative efficiency increases to a maximum of 3.7 when change is roughly 1.0 $\sigma/\sqrt{n}$ and at each end of range the limiting values are 1.0.

Table 8.1 Relative efficiency of detection of control schemes

Change in process average (in multiples of $\sigma/\sqrt{n}$)	Shewhart A.R.L. to detection	CuSum A.R.L. to detection	Relative efficiency in detecting changes
0	500	500	1.0
0.5	100	30	3.3
1.0	33	9.0	3.7
1.5	12	5.0	2.4
2.0	5.2	3.0	1.7
2.5	2.8	2.1	1.3
2.88	2.0	1.7	1.2

Table 8.2 Comparison of attribute control schemes (ARLs at A.Q.L. $L_0 = 500$)

Value of m_1	CuSum A.R.L. = 2			CuSum A.R.L. = 5			CuSum A.R.L. = 10		
	m_2	Shewhart A.R.L.	Relative sensitivity (ϵ)	m_2	Shewhart A.R.L.	Relative sensitivity (ϵ)	m_2	Shewhart A.R.L.	Relative sensitivity (ϵ)
0.51	3.40	2.30	1.15	2.10	6.20	1.2	1.60	12.7	1.3
2.16	7.18	2.30	1.15	5.15	6.40	1.3	4.32	14.10	1.4
3.24	9.22	2.30	1.15	6.26	9.60	1.9	5.29	22.7	2.7
3.89	10.28	1.84	0.92	7.24	8.80	1.8	6.20	19.5	2.0
7.04	16.00	1.90	0.95	11.25	9.30	1.9	9.80	23.7	2.37
10.00	21.06	1.89	0.95	14.98	12.05	2.4	13.15	40.0	4.00

Thus the CuSum control is always superior to the Shewhart control system and its relative efficiency depends on the magnitude of the change — at best the CuSum is approximately 4 times more efficient at detecting changes than the Shewhart system, while both schemes are comparable at very small and/or very large changes.

8.3   Attribute Control: Comparison of CuSum and Shewhart Schemes

As with the variable schemes, the comparison of the attribute schemes has been made with the same A.R.L.s to detection, namely $L_0 = 500$, for both CuSum and Shewhart schemes. The comparison is given over ranges of values of m_1 average defects/sample at A.Q.L. Table 9* has been used to obtain the A.R.L.s to detection for the CuSum schemes, while A.R.L.s for the Shewhart schemes have been calculated using table 1* (with the same values of m_2).

The comparison of the schemes is again by

$$\text{Relative efficiency of detection } (\epsilon) = \frac{\text{A.R.L. of Shewhart scheme}}{\text{A.R.L. of CuSum scheme}}$$

The comparison is given in table 8.2 for A.R.L.s for CuSum of $L_1 = 2, L_1 = 5$ and $L_1 = 10$.

In the calculation of the Shewhart A.R.L., the detection limit has been chosen to give nearest value to $L_0 = 500$. Since however only integral values are possible values of m_1 have been chosen for table 8.2 to ensure that Shewhart A.R.L.s are also approximately equal to 500.

Table 8.2 again shows similar results as obtained in the comparison of variable charts namely that in the detection of major changes, the schemes are similar.

Referring to table 8.2 for A.R.L. of 2 of detection for the CuSum, the Shewhart A.R.L.s are comparable.

Again with CuSum A.R.L. of 10, the Shewhart A.R.L. are up to 4 times as large.

Thus as with variable charts, CuSum attribute charts are more efficient at detecting changes than Shewhart charts and the improvement in efficiency depends on the magnitude of the change — an improvement of up to 4 being obtained in the relative sensitivity of the schemes — similar to results on variable charts.

8.4   Selection of Control Scheme in Practice (Shewhart versus CuSum)

While the CuSum control charts are clearly superior to Shewhart charts in their efficiency in detecting changes in process average, there are many other factors to be taken into account in selecting a quality control scheme.

The Shewhart charts are simpler to construct and very much easier to understand. It is this factor, namely the ease of interpretation together with the fact that the charts for effective control require to be understood by all personnel involved including the process operator, manager, inspector, etc., that makes the use of CuSum charts not suitable for shop floor use.

Although, with education and time, the use of CuSum charts will increase, the author recommends that for control of processes, the Shewhart charts should still be adopted with CuSum techniques best used for analysis and diagnosis of special control problems.

9. Introduction to Sampling Inspection—Single Attribute Schemes

9.1 Introduction

The quality control systems described in this book are usually linked in practice to sampling inspection schemes. These inspection schemes are required as an additional safety check on the control system since as was clearly illustrated no process control chart can ensure that it detects immediately when a process goes *out of control*, i.e. there is a finite run length before detection. Therefore, sampling inspection is carried out before finally accepting the product. Again there is a need for inspecting incoming products into the factory and sampling inspection schemes are used to ensure greater control over the quality levels accepted into the factory.

This chapter gives readers an introduction to the basic concepts of sampling inspection by considering in full the design of single attribute sampling inspection schemes. References are given at the end of the chapter to where details can be obtained on the design of other attribute schemes and variable sampling schemes.

9.2 Sampling Inspection Versus 100% Inspection Schemes

The three functions of inspection can be classified as follows:

(1) To sort articles into good and bad.
(2) To assess the quality level of the process which produced the items.
(3) To provide the manufacturer with an incentive to produce a good quality product.

Of these, the first can only be accomplished by 100% inspection, but it should be remembered that 100% inspection by human operators is rarely 100% effective.

The second function can be carried out either by 100% inspection or by sampling inspection. However, if the prime function of the 100% inspection is to sort the items, then the quality level may be overlooked and in this respect, sampling is often better.

Thirdly, if the manufacturer or manufacturing department knows that 100%

106

inspection of his product is regarded by the user merely as a sorting out process then he has no great incentive to keep his quality level high. This is clearly undesirable and sampling inspection by the consumer should have the effect of producing this incentive to improve quality, providing rejections are made when appropriate.

Thus, it will be seen that even without any additional outside constraints such as cost, etc., sampling inspection schemes have advantages over 100% inspection schemes.

In practice, there are in addition many factors which necessitate the use of sampling inspection rather than 100% inspection, including:

(i) The cost of inspection – 100% inspection cost may be prohibitive.

(ii) If the inspection is a destructive test, clearly 100% inspection is not feasible.

9.3 Basic Concepts of a Sampling Plan

Inspection may be carried out on an attribute or on a measurement basis and there are various types of plan for each of these categories.

To demonstrate the use of sampling schemes, in this chapter the design of single sampling plans using an attribute classification is given.

The inspection schemes for measurement control have similar features and references to their design are given at the end of the chapter.

It is assumed that the product to be inspected is grouped into discrete batches either physically in separate containers, or distinguishable in some other way. Also that the sample size is less than 10% of batch size, i.e. ($n < 0.10N$).

Suppose that the batches are each of size N (note that in practice the batches do not have to be of equal size) and the quality (percentage defective) of each batch is to be assessed in order to decide whether to accept or reject the batch.

The rules of the single sample scheme are simple; take *random* samples of n items from the batch and determine the number of defective items in the sample. If this observed number of defectives is *less than* or *equal* to some pre-assigned number, c, *accept* the batch. If it is *more than* c, *reject* the batch. The fate of rejected batches is at the moment unspecified.

Since the batch is being sentenced on a sample evidence, it can never be certain that the correct decision has been made, i.e. there is always a chance that poor quality batches will be accepted and a chance that batches of good quality will be rejected.

A requirement of the plan, therefore, is that these two risks inherent in the decision process based on sample data should be set at some specified (small) values. In order to do this, the choice of the parameters, n and c, of the plan cannot be arbitrary and there are various methods of selecting these numbers according to what is required of the sampling inspection process.

9.4   The Features of a Sampling Inspection Scheme

Basically, there are six features of a sampling plan, selection of any two of which will uniquely specify the properties of the scheme. They are:

(1) The sample size, n.
(2) The acceptance number, c.
(3) The quality of batch which is 'almost certain' of acceptance, p_1.
(4) The quality of batch which is 'almost certain' of rejection, p_2.
(5) The average outgoing quality limit (A.O.Q.L.).
(6) The average amount of inspection per batch, I.

Properties 1 – 4 apply to all sampling inspection and 5 and 6 to non-destructive testing.

Features 1 and 2 are self explanatory, and in 3 and 4, 'almost certain' is determined by the risks of making the wrong decision for the given batch quality. These risks are usually less than 10% in magnitude.

Feature 5, the average outgoing quality limit (A.O.Q.L.), is the limiting or maximum value of the average quality (percentage defective) of batches which will be obtained after inspection regardless of incoming quality.

The A.O.Q.L. is based on:

(i) All rejected batches are 100% inspected and defective items found are replaced with good items.

(ii) The efficiency of the 100% inspection is perfect.

These screened batches, theoretically of perfect quality, are then passed into store along with accepted batches, which will contain some defectives. Figure 9.1 illustrates this inspection process.

Thus if probability of rejecting a batch $= P(R)$
and probability of accepting a batch $= P(A) = 1 - P(R)$
then the average outgoing quality[†] (A.O.Q.) $= p \times P(A)$
The average outgoing quality limit (A.O.Q.L.) is the maximum value of the outgoing quality level.

Feature 6, the average amount of inspection per batch, assuming that rejected batches are 100% inspected, is given by:

Average amount of inspection batch $(I) = n + (N - n) P(R)$

[†]The formula given here for the outgoing quality level (A.O.Q.) is approximate only and depends on the batch size (N) being large in comparison to the sample size n.

Since a sample of size n is drawn from the batch, if the batch is accepted then the true

$$\text{Fraction effective/batch} = p \, \frac{(N - n)}{N}$$

and the average outgoing quality $= p \, \frac{(N - p)}{N} \times P(A)$

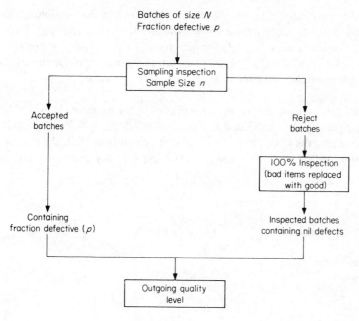

Figure 9.1

9.5 The Operating Characteristic (O.C.) Curve of a Sampling Plan

The operating characteristic curve shows how well, or otherwise, the sampling plan discriminates between batches of good and bad quality submitted to inspection.

Let the quality level up to which the consumer is prepared to accept, be p_1, known as the acceptable quality level, i.e. all batches submitted to inspection with equal or less defective level should be accepted, while all batches whose quality level is worse than p_1, should be rejected.

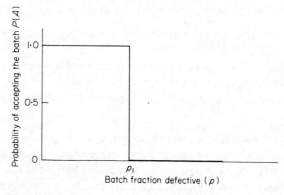

Figure 9.2 Operating characteristic curve for perfect inspection

Diagrammatically, this requirement can be shown in the relationship between the probability of accepting the batch $P(A)$ and the batch quality p. Thus figure 9.2 shows the perfect relationship, namely a probability of *one* of accepting batches with fraction defective up to p_1, and a probability of *zero* of accepting batches with fraction defective greater than p_1.

Clearly this perfect inspection system could only be achieved by 100% inspection and if this inspection is also 100% efficient.

In practice, the O.C. curve would be as shown in figure 9.3, the sharp corners being rounded due to the sampling errors implicit in any sampling plan.

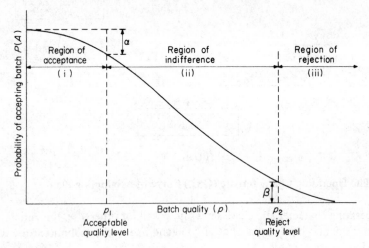

Figure 9.3

Referring to figure 9.3.

α = 'risk' or probability of rejecting batches of acceptable quality level p_1.

β = 'risk' or probability of accepting batches of reject quality level p_2.

It will also be seen that the O.C. curve is divided in the regions:

(i) *Acceptance region* — the range of batch quality that is 'almost certain' to be accepted.

(ii) *Indifference region* — the range of batch quality that can either be accepted or rejected, dependent on chance.

(iii) *Rejection region* – the range of batch quality that is almost certain to be rejected.

The risks 'α' and 'β', known in inspection sampling, as the 'producers' and 'consumers' risks respectively are set usually below the level of 0.10 and in practice levels of either 0.01, 0.05 or 0.10 are generally used. Clearly it is also desirable to keep the indifference region small and increasing the sample size has the effect of reducing this region.

Each sampling plan has an O.C. curve and this is uniquely determined by predetermining any two of the first four features of the plan.

Thus the given values of n and c will uniquely determine an inspection plan as will the fixing of risks α and β for the given quality levels p_1 and p_2.

9.6 Design of a Sampling Plan

9.6.1 Method 1 – Given Values of n and c

It is possible to obtain the value for the O.C. curve directly from table 10* but in this first example the curve will be derived from the Poisson distribution – an assumption implicit in all designs here is that the batch quality is less than 10% defective for the Poisson approximation to be used and $n \leqslant 0.10N$ – if in practice the sample size is greater than 10% of the batch size, the design of the sampling inspection scheme is complicated by the fact that the hypergeometric distribution must be used.

Example

Sample size $n = 100$, an acceptable number, $c = 2$, batch size $N = 10\,000$, acceptable quality level = 0.01

Consider now a range of batch quality levels.

Let $p = 0.01$. Thus, if batches of $p = 0.01$ are submitted then: direct from table 1* (with $m = np = 100 \times 0.01 = 1$)
Probability of rejecting $P(R)$ = Probability of obtaining 3 or more defects in sample of $n = 100$ =   0.0803
Therefore probability of accepting $P(A)$ = 0.9197

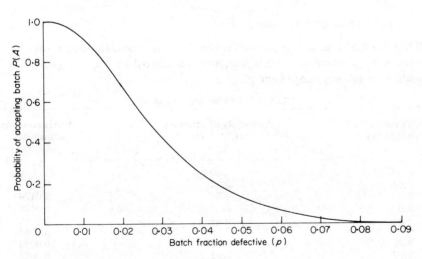

Figure 9.4 Operating characteristic curve ($n = 100$, $c = 2$, $N = 10\,000$)

Again $p = 0.005$ Probability of rejecting $P(R) = 0.0144$ therefore $P(A) = 0.9856$
       $p = 0.02$ Probability of rejecting $P(R) = 0.0323$ therefore $P(A) = 0.6767$
       $p = 0.03$ Probability of rejecting $P(R) = 0.5768$ therefore $P(A) = 0.3232$
       $p = 0.04$ Probability of rejecting $P(R) = 0.7619$ therefore $P(A) = 0.2381$
       $p = 0.05$ Probability of rejecting $P(R) = 0.8753$ therefore $P(A) = 0.1247$
       $p = 0.06$ Probability of rejecting $P(R) = 0.9380$ therefore $P(A) = 0.0620$
       $p = 0.07$ Probability of rejecting $P(R) = 0.9704$ therefore $P(A) = 0.0296$

This O.C. curve is show in figure 9.4.

Alternative Method Using Table 10*

Here the probability of accepting $P(A)$ is read directly off table 10* and the values
of np are obtained from the table.
    Thus when $P(A) = 0.500$ $np = 2.67$
Therefore batch fraction defective $p = 2.67/100 = 0.0267$
Similarly

$P(A)$	np	p
0.975	0.619	0.006
0.95	0.818	0.008
0.75	1.727	0.017
0.50	2.674	0.027
0.25	3.920	0.039
0.05	6.290	0.063
0.01	8.406	0.084

giving the same O.C. curve as before.

Average Outgoing Quality Limit (A.O.Q.L.)

If it is assumed that all rejected batches are 100% screened, all defects being
replaced by good ones, then it is possible to calculate the average outgoing
quality for any incoming batch quality.

Table 9.1 Average outgoing quality

Batch fraction defective (p)	Probability of accepting batch ($P(A)$)	Average outgoing quality (A.O.Q.)
0	1.00	0
0.01	0.92	0.0092
0.02	0.67	0.0134
0.03	0.42	0.0126
0.04	0.24	0.0096
0.05	0.13	0.0065
0.06	0.06	0.0036
0.07	0.03	0.0021
0.08	0.01	0.0008

For example for batch fraction defective $p = 0.02$, from figure 9.4 $P(A) = 0.67$
Therefore average outgoing quality A.O.Q. $= 0.02 \times 0.67 = 0.0134$
Table 9.1 gives the values of the A.O.Q. for a range of batch defective.

Thus the average outgoing quality limit (A.O.Q.L.), which is the maximum value of the A.O.Q., is approximately 0.0134, or 1.34% defective. Thus in this sampling plan, the average outgoing quality will never exceed 1.34%.

Average amount of inspection per batch

The average amount of inspection per batch depends on the incoming quality level. For the average incoming quality level of 0.01,

$$I = 100 + (10\ 000 - 100)\ 0.0803$$
$$= 100 + 795$$
$$= 895$$

It is interesting to note that it is doubtful if this scheme would be acceptable in practice because of the high level of average inspection per batch; approx. 9% of the batch.

9.6.2   Method 2 – Calculation of the Plan Which Minimises Average Total Inspection per batch

Assumed given the batch size (N), acceptable quality level (A.Q.L.) and one point on the operating characteristic curve.

Example

Batch size $N = 1500$
Acceptable quality level (A.Q.L.) = 1%
    Requirement that if batches of 6% defective are submitted, they only have a 10% chance of being accepted.
    Determine the sampling plan to minimise the average total inspection per batch.
    There is a possible sampling plan to satisfy the constraints for each acceptance number (c).
    Consider a range of acceptance numbers and corresponding O.C. curves.
Table 9.2 sets out the tabulation for finding the 'best' plan. The calculations for constructing table 9.2 are given below.
    Column (2), the value of m is obtained from table 1*, the cumulative Poisson tables. For example for $c = 1$, the chance of finding 2 or more defects in the sample must be 0.90 or a 10% chance of accepting the batch when the batch fraction defective (p) is 0.06. Thus from table 1* $m = 3.9$ gives probability (of 2 or more defects) = 0.9008 (the closest value to 0.9000).
    Then the sample size n is determined by
$$m = 3.9 = np = n \times 0.06$$

Table 9.2 Average total inspection per batch (I) for range of values of acceptance No. (c)

Acceptance No. (c) (1)	Expected average No. of defects (m) (2)	Sample size (n) (n=m/0.06) (3)	Probability of rejection at $p = 0.01$ (P(R)) (4)	Average total inspection per batch ($I = n + (N-n)P(R)$) (5)
0	2.3	38	0.316	499
1	3.9	65	0.139	264
2	5.3	88	0.060	171
3	6.7	112	0.027	150
4	8.0	133	0.012	149
5	9.3	155	0.005	162
.	.	.	.	.
.	.	.	.	.

or sample size $n = m/0.06 = 3.9/0.06 = 65$

For input of batch quality of 0.01

Average defects/sample $= n \times 0.01 = 0.65$

Therefore from table 1* $m = 0.65$

Probability of 2 or more defects $= 0.139$ (interpolation)

Therefore average total inspection/batch $= 65 + (1500-65) \, 0.139 = 264$

Selection of Sampling Plan

Reference to table 9.2 shows that $c = 4$ gives the lowest average total inspection per batch giving a sampling scheme with $n = 133, c = 4$.

It should be noted that plan $n = 112, c = 3$ is almost equivalent. In practice either plan is acceptable, but $n = 133, c = 4$ gives a marginally lower A.O.Q.L. and therefore has been chosen here, see below.

Table 9.3

Probability of accepting batch ($P(A)$)	Value of np (from table 9*)	Batch fraction defective (p)	Average outgoing quality ($P(A) \times p$)
0.99	1.279	0.0096	0.0096
0.95	1.970	0.0148	0.0140
0.90	2.433	0.0183	0.0167
0.75	3.369	0.0253	0.0189
0.50	4.671	0.0351	0.0175
0.25	6.274	0.0479	0.0118
0.10	7.994	0.0601	0.006
0.05	9.154	0.0688	0.0034
0.01	11.605	0.0872	0.0008

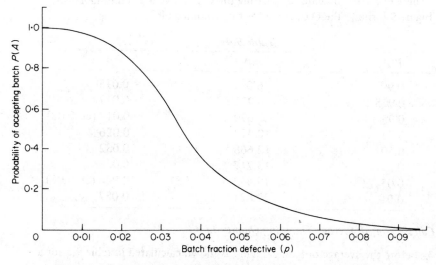

Figure 9.5 Operating characteristic curve ($n = 133, c = 4, N = 1500$)

Determination of O.C. Curve and Outgoing Quality Level

Using table 10*, the calculation of the O.C. curve is given in table 9.3. This operating characteristic curve is shown in figure 9.5.

9.6.3   Method 3 -- Given Values of P_1, P_2, and α and β

The defining of any two points on the O.C. curve uniquely determines the sampling plan. It is usual to give the values of acceptable quality level, (p_1) and reject quality level, (p_2) with their associated risks (α) and (β).

Example

Calculate the sampling plan which:

(i) has a risk of 5% of rejecting batches of quality 2% or under;
(ii) has a risk of 5% of accepting batches of quality level 5% or over.

Here acceptable quality level $p_1 = 0.02$ $\alpha = 0.05$
Reject quality level $p_2 = 0.05$ $\beta = 0.05$
$\therefore R = p_2/p_1 = 0.05/0.02 = 2.5$
Referring to table 9* for $\alpha = 0.05$ and $\beta = 0.05$
Acceptance No. $c = 12$ with $np_1 = 7.690$ (for $p_2/p_1 = 2.528$ in table 10*)
Sample size $n = 7.690/0.02 = 384.5 \doteq 400$
Thus a sampling plan, $n = 400$, $c = 12$ will give a 5% risk of rejecting batches of 2% defective while giving also a 5% risk of accepting batches of 5% defective.

Calculation of O.C. Curve

Using table 10*, the data for plotting the O.C. curve is given in table 9.4. Figure 9.6 shows the O.C. curve for this sampling plan.

Table 9.4

P(A)	np	p
0.99	6.099	0.015
0.975	6.922	0.017
0.95	7.690	0.019 (cf. 0.02)
0.75	10.422	0.026
0.50	12.668	0.032
0.25	15.217	0.038
0.05	19.442	0.048 (cf. 0.05)
0.01	22.821	0.057

Calculation of Average Outgoing Quality Limit

As before the average outgoing quality is shown calculated in table 9.5 for a range of batch fraction defective.

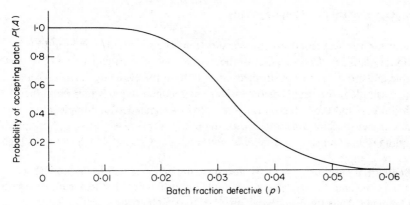

Figure 9.6 Operating characteristic curve ($n = 400, c = 12$)

Table 9.5 Average outgoing quality

Batch fraction defective (p)	Probability of † accepting batch ($P(A)$)	Average outgoing quality (A.O.Q.)
0.01	0.999	0.01
0.015	0.99	0.015
0.02	0.93	0.018
0.025	0.78	0.0195
0.03	0.58	0.017
0.04	0.19	0.007
0.05	0.04	0.002

† From figure 9.5.

Thus the average outgoing quality (A.O.Q.), has a maximum value of approximately 0.02, whatever the quality level going into the plan, or the A.O.Q.L. = 0.02.

Average Amount of Inspection per Batch

Clearly this plan will only be feasible if there is a low probability of rejection of incoming batches thus giving a low average amount of inspection per batch.

Thus if incoming quality level is below 0.02, this scheme is feasible but otherwise an alternative scheme should be designed to reduce the inspection required.

When using this method to design a sampling plan, the average incoming quality level should be below the acceptable quality level (p_1).

For example if batch size $N = 5000$ then for an incoming quality level of 0.015

Average amount of inspection/batch $I = 400 + (5000 - 400)(1 - 0.99) = 446$

However if incoming quality level is 0.030, then average amount of inspection/batch $I = 400 + (5000 - 400)(1 - 0.58) = 2332$

or approx 50% of total product — not a suitable inspection plan.

9.7   Other Attribute Sampling Plans

In addition to these single attribute inspection schemes, double and multiple attribute plans are also available. In the double plan, the scheme is to take a first sample and either (i) accept or reject the batch on the evidence or (ii) take a second sample if the first is inconclusive. The second sample is then combined with the first and the batch is either accepted or rejected after comparison of the total number of defectives found with the pre-set acceptance number. Multiple sampling is an extension of double to any number of stages, which can be as high as seven or eight.

Sequential sampling plans have also been devised whereby items are inspected one at a time and the evidence is accumulated until a decision to accept or reject can be made. Thus the cumulative proportion of defectives found to items inspected is compared after the inspection of every item with pre-assigned values, a decision being made either to accept the batch, reject the batch or to sample another item.

It is usually possible to select the parameters of any of these types of plan so that they all have equivalent O.C. curves (and thus give the equivalent protection to the consumer and producer). The choice of one type rather than another is usually fixed by such factors as administrative convenience, economy of sampling effort, etc.

9.8   Variable Sampling Plans

It is also possible to devise plans similar to the above, i.e. single, double, sequential, where measurements are made rather than using the attribute classification and a number of references are given at the end of this chapter to books which discuss variable sampling plans.

9.9   Ministry of Defence Sampling Plans – Military Standard 105D

Standard military sampling plans for attribute inspection were developed during World War II and a Military Standard 105D was issued by the U.S. Government in 1963. This standard has been adopted by the International Organisation for Standardisation as International Standard ISO/DIS-2859.

These tables are therefore widely used for setting up attribute sampling plans and readers are referred to this Military Standard – see reference No. 9 at the end of this chapter.

9.10   Problems for Solution – Single Attribute Sampling Plans

(1)   A single-sample attribute sampling plan is required with the following:

(a)   Risk of rejecting batches with fraction defective 0.02 or less to be 5%.

(b) Risk of accepting batches with fraction defective 0.10 or more is to be 5%.

(i) Find the required values for the sample size and the acceptance number.

(ii) What is the probability of accepting batches with fraction defective of 0.07?

(iii) What is the batch fraction defective which has a 50% chance of being accepted?

(iv) Under the sampling plan designed what will be the average amount of inspection per batch with an incoming quality level of 0.03 fraction defective, given the batch size 2000.

(2) An acceptance sampling plan operates as follows:

(a) A random sample of 100 items is drawn from each batch and inspected.

(b) The batch is accepted if 3 or fewer defectives are found.

(c) If 4 or more defectives are found, inspect the entire batch and replace all defective items with good.

All batches contain 1200 items.

(i) Determine the operating characteristics curve of this plan and estimate the average outgoing quality limit.

(ii) If incoming lots are 3% defective, what will be the average amount of inspection per batch?

(3) Batches of size N = 10 000 are submitted for sampling inspection. Given:

(a) that the average incoming quality level is 3%;

(b) that, if batches of 7% defective are submitted, these batches should have only a 1% chance of being accepted;
Design the sampling inspection scheme to give minimum average inspection/batch.

(4) Inspection of batches received from a supplier has established that the average incoming quality is 3% with a standard deviation of 0.25% – normally distributed.

Design a single attribute sampling plan to:

(a) 5% risk of rejecting batches of 3% or less;

(b) 5% risk of accepting batches of 8% or over.

What percentage of batches can the producer expect to be rejected?

9.11   Solution to Problems

No. 1

Here $p_1 = 0.02$, $\alpha = 0.05$
$p_2 = 0.10$, $\beta = 0.05$

Therefore $R = \dfrac{p_2}{p_1} = \dfrac{0.10}{0.02} = 5.0$

(a) Referring to table 10*

it gives for $c = 3, np_1 = 1.366$, ratio of $\dfrac{p_2}{p_1} = 5.675$

and $c = 4, np_1 = 1.970$, ratio of $\dfrac{p_2}{p_1} = 4.46$

Taking the value greater than 5 gives the acceptance no. $c = 3$, and sample size

$n = \dfrac{1.366}{0.02} = 68.3 \doteqdot 70$

(b) If batch fraction defective $(p) = 0.07$ then average defects/sample m = $np = 70 \times 0.07 = 4.9$

Referring to table 1* for $m = 4.9$, the probability of accepting batches of 0.07 fraction defective = probability of less than 4 defects = 1 – probability (of 4 or more) = $1 - 0.7207 = 0.2793$

(c) For $n = 70, c = 3$ and $P(A) = 0.50$, reference to table 11* gives $np = 3.672$ where p = batch fraction defective with 50% chance of being accepted. Batch fraction defective $(p) = 3.672/70 = 0.052$ fraction defective which has a 50% chance of being accepted.

(d) Incoming quality level = 0.03, batch size $n = 2000$

Table 1*, $m = np = 70 \times 0.03 = 2.1$

therefore probability of accepting batches $P(A) = 1 - 0.1614 = 0.84$

Therefore average amount of inspection/batch $I = n + (N-n) P(R) = 70 + (2000-70) (1-0.84) = 70 + 309.0 = 379.0$ or over 1/3 of the components. Clearly in practice this scheme would not be satisfactory with this level of incoming quality.

No. 2

(a) Here $n = 100, c = 3, N = 1200$. From table 10*, table 9.6 can be compiled.

Table 9.6

P(A)	np	p
0.99	0.823	0.008
0.975	1.090	0.011
0.95	1.366	0.014
0.75	2.535	0.025
0.50	3.672	0.037
0.25	5.109	0.051
0.05	7.750	0.078
0.01	10.045	0.100

Figure 9.7 gives the O.C. curve for the sampling plan. From figure 9.7, table 9.7 can be obtained.

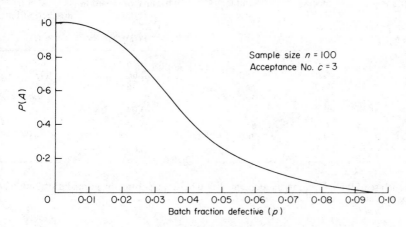

Figure 9.7 Operating characteristic curve ($n = 100$, $c = 3$)

Table 9.7 Average outgoing quality

Batch fraction defect (p)	Probability of accepting batch $P(A)$	Average † outgoing quality (A.O.Q.)
0.01	0.98	0.010
0.02	0.85	0.017
0.03	0.64	0.019
0.04	0.44	0.017
0.05	0.26	0.013
0.06	0.16	0.010

† A.O.Q. $= P(A) \times p$

Thus the average outgoing quality limit (A.O.Q.L.) = 0.019 or 2% approximately.

(b) Incoming batch fraction defective = 0.03. The probability of accepting batches with $p = 0.03$, $P(A) = 0.64$ (from table 9.7)
Therefore average amount of inspection/shipment $I = 100 + (1200-100) \, 0.36$
$= 100 + 396 = 496 \doteq 500$ an excessive amount.

Referring to figure 9.7 the incoming quality level should be below 1.5% for satisfactory operation of this inspection scheme.

No.3

$N = 10\ 000$. Average incoming batch fraction defective = 0.03
Given a probability of accepting batches of 7% defective of 0.01 table 9.8 can be set out.

Table 9.8

Acceptance (c)	Expected No. of defects (m)	Sample size (n)	Probability of rejection at p = 0.03 (P(R))	Average inspection/batch (I)
0	4.6	65	0.86	8609
2	8.4	120	0.69	6937
8	18.0	257	0.36	3764
16	28.0	400	0.10	1360
24	40.0	57	0.04	948
30	46.0[1]	657	0.02	833
32	49.0	700	0.009	784*
34	51.1	730	0.006	786

[1] Here the use of table 1* has to be replaced with table 2*, i.e. using the normal distribution as an approximation to the Poisson distribution

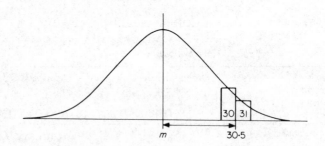

Figure 9.8 Use of normal approximation

In using the normal distribution the values of m are obtained as shown in figure 9.8, where $c = 30$.

Given that for $p = 0.07$ the probability of obtaining 31 or more defects is 0.01. Then

$$\frac{30.5 - m}{\sqrt{m}} = 2.33 \quad \text{and} \quad m - 2.33\sqrt{m} - 30.5 = 0$$

Therefore

$$\sqrt{m} = \frac{+2.33 \pm \sqrt{(2.33^2 + 4 \times 30.5)}}{2}$$

$$= \frac{2.33 + 11.3}{2} = 6.815$$

Therefore expected defects/sample $m = 6.815^2 = 46$

Reference to table 9.8 shows that the minimum average inspection per batch is obtained with a sampling plan, $c = 32, n = 700$.

No. 4

Here $p_1 = 0.03$ $\alpha = 0.05$ $p_2 = 0.08$ $\beta = 0.05$

Therefore $R = \dfrac{p_2}{p_1} = \dfrac{0.08}{0.03} = 2.67$

From table 10* acceptance No. $c = 10, np_1 = 6.169$

Therefore sample size $n = \dfrac{6.169}{0.03} \doteqdot 205.9 \doteqdot 200$

Sampling plan $n = 200, c = 10$ gives the required design.
The operating characteristic curve parameters are given in table 9.9.

Table 9.9

P(A)	np	p
0.995	4.320	0.0216
0.99	4.771	0.0238
0.975	5.491	0.0275
0.95	6.169	0.0308
0.90	7.021	0.0351
0.75	8.620	0.0431
0.50	10.668	0.0533
0.25	13.020	0.0650
0.05	16.962	0.0848
0.01	20.145	0.1072

The probability distribution of incoming quality level is given in figure 9.9.

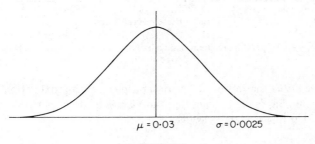

$\mu = 0{\cdot}03$ $\sigma = 0{\cdot}0025$

Figure 9.9

Table 9.10 gives the probability of occurrence of batches of various quality levels.

Therefore probability of any batch being rejected $= 0.0214 \times 0.01 + 0.1356 \times 0.02 + 0.3413 \times 0.035 + \ldots + 0.02275 \times 0.12 = 0.047$
or approximately a 5% chance of being rejected.

Table 9.10

Incoming quality class interval	Quality level (mid-point)	Probability †	Probability †† of this batch quality being accepted ($P(A)$)
0.0225 – 0.0250	0.02375	0.0214	0.99
0.0250 – 0.0275	0.02625	0.1356	0.98
0.0275 – 0.0300	0.02875	0.3413	0.965
0.0300 – 0.0325	0.03125	0.3413	0.945
0.0325 – 0.0350	0.03375	0.1498	0.92
0.0350 – 0.0375	0.03625	0.0919	0.88
0.0375 –	0.03875		

† From table 2*.
†† From O.C. curve (figure 9.10 shows the O.C. curve over the range 0.02 – 0.04 of batch fraction defective).

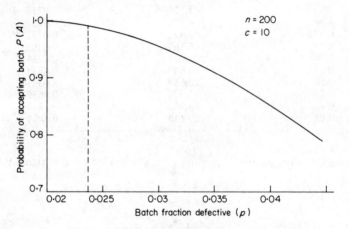

Figure 9.10 Operating characteristic curve over range $p = 0.02 - 0.04$
($n = 200, c = 10$)

It should be noted that for most practical purposes an approximation can be obtained by assuming for all batches that the average quality level is 3%. Readers should check that this gives 4.2% as rejection rate.

References

Readers are referred to the following books for further details on the design of other attribute schemes and the design of variable sampling inspection schemes.

Sampling Inspection Schemes

1. E. L. Grant (1972). *Statistical Quality Control.* McGraw-Hill, New York
2. A. J. Duncan (1974). *Quality Control and Industrial Statistics.* Irwin, New York

3. A. Ward (1947). *Sequential Analysis.* Wiley, New York
4. J. M. Juran *et al.* (1974). *Quality Control Handbook.* McGraw-Hill, New York
5.   Bowker and   Goode ( ) *Sampling by Variables.*
6.   Freeman *et al.* ( ). *Sampling Inspection (Attrib.).*

Sampling Inspection Tables

7. BS.6001 (1955). *Sampling Procedures and Tables for Inspection by Attributes.*
   British Standards Institution, London (equivalent to Reference 9)
8. H. F. Dodge and H. G. Romig (1959). *Sampling Inspection Tables.* Wiley,
   New York
9. MIL-STD-105D, Military Standard. *Sampling Procedures and Tables for
   Inspection by Attributes.* U.S. Dept. of Defense
10. MIL-STD-414, *Military Standard Sampling Procedures and Tables for Inspection by Variables.* U.S. Dept. of Defense

Appendix: Statistical Tables

Table 1 Cumulative Poisson Probabilities

The table gives the probability that r or more random events are contained in an interval when the average number of such events per interval is m, i.e.

$$\sum_{x=r}^{\infty} e^{-m}\, \frac{m^x}{x!}$$

Where there is no entry for a particular pair of values of r and m, this indicates that the appropriate probability is less than 0.000 05. Similarly, except for the case r = 0 when the entry is exact, a tabulated value of 1.0000 represents a probability greater than 0.999 95.

m =	0.1	0.2	0.3	0.4	0.5	0.6	0.7	0.8	0.9	1.0
r = 0	1.0000	1.0000	1.0000	1.0000	1.0000	1.0000	1.0000	1.0000	1.0000	1.0000
1	.0952	.1813	.2592	.3297	.3935	.4512	.5034	.5507	.5934	.6321
2	.0047	.0175	.0369	.0616	.0902	.1219	.1558	.1912	.2275	.2642
3	.0002	.0011	.0036	.0079	.0144	.0231	.0341	.0474	.0629	.0803
4		.0001	.0003	.0008	.0018	.0034	.0058	.0091	.0135	.0190
5				.0001	.0002	.0004	.0008	.0014	.0023	.0037
6							.0001	.0002	.0003	.0006
7										.0001

$m =$	1.1	1.2	1.3	1.4	1.5	1.6	1.7	1.8	1.9	2.0
$r = 0$	1.0000	1.0000	1.0000	1.0000	1.0000	1.0000	1.0000	1.0000	1.0000	1.0000
1	.6671	.6988	.7275	.7534	.7769	.7981	.8173	.8347	.8504	.8647
2	.3010	.3374	.3732	.4082	.4422	.4751	.5068	.5372	.5663	.5940
3	.0996	.1205	.1429	.1665	.1912	.2166	.2428	.2694	.2963	.3233
4	.0257	.0338	.0431	.0537	.0656	.0788	.0932	.1087	.1253	.1429
5	.0054	.0077	.0107	.0143	.0186	.0237	.0296	.0364	.0441	.0527
6	.0010	.0015	.0022	.0032	.0045	.0060	.0080	.0104	.0132	.0166
7	.0001	.0003	.0004	.0006	.0009	.0013	.0019	.0026	.0034	.0045
8			.0001	.0001	.0002	.0003	.0004	.0006	.0008	.0011
9							.0001	.0001	.0002	.0002

$m =$	2.1	2.2	2.3	2.4	2.5	2.6	2.7	2.8	2.9	3.0
$r = 0$	1.0000	1.0000	1.0000	1.0000	1.0000	1.0000	1.0000	1.0000	1.0000	1.0000
1	.8775	.8892	.8997	.9093	.9179	.9257	.9328	.9392	.9450	.9502
2	.6204	.6454	.6691	.6916	.7127	.7326	.7513	.7689	.7854	.8009
3	.3504	.3773	.4040	.4303	.4562	.4816	.5064	.5305	.5540	.5768
4	.1614	.1806	.2007	.2213	.2424	.2640	.2859	.3081	.3304	.3528
5	.0621	.0725	.0838	.0959	.1088	.1226	.1371	.1523	.1682	.1847
6	.0204	.0249	.0300	.0357	.0420	.0490	.0567	.0651	.0742	.0839
7	.0059	.0075	.0094	.0116	.0142	.0172	.0206	.0244	.0287	.0335
8	.0015	.0020	.0026	.0033	.0042	.0053	.0066	.0081	.0099	.0119
9	.0003	.0005	.0006	.0009	.0011	.0015	.0019	.0024	.0031	.0038
10	.0001	.0001	.0001	.0002	.0003	.0004	.0005	.0007	.0009	.0011
11					.0001	.0001	.0001	.0002	.0002	.0003
12								.0001	.0001	.0001

Table 1 continued Cumulative Poisson Probabilities

m =	3.1	3.2	3.3	3.4	3.5	3.6	3.7	3.8	3.9	4.0
r = 0	1.0000	1.0000	1.0000	1.0000	1.0000	1.0000	1.0000	1.0000	1.0000	1.0000
1	.9550	.9592	.9631	.9666	.9698	.9727	.9753	.9776	.9798	.9817
2	.8153	.8288	.8414	.8532	.8641	.8743	.8838	.8926	.9008	.9084
3	.5988	.6201	.6406	.6603	.6792	.6973	.7146	.7311	.7469	.7619
4	.3752	.3975	.4197	.4416	.4634	.4848	.5058	.5265	.5468	.5665
5	.2018	.2194	.2374	.2558	.2746	.2936	.3128	.3322	.3516	.3712
6	.0943	.1054	.1171	.1295	.1424	.1559	.1699	.1844	.1994	.2149
7	.0388	.0446	.0510	.0579	.0653	.0733	.0818	.0909	.1005	.1107
8	.0142	.0168	.0198	.0231	.0267	.0308	.0352	.0401	.0454	.0511
9	.0047	.0057	.0069	.0083	.0099	.0117	.0137	.0160	.0185	.0214
10	.0014	.0018	.0022	.0027	.0033	.0040	.0048	.0058	.0069	.0081
11	.0004	.0005	.0006	.0008	.0010	.0013	.0016	.0019	.0023	.0028
12	.0001	.0001	.0002	.0002	.0003	.0004	.0005	.0006	.0007	.0009
13				.0001	.0001	.0001	.0001	.0002	.0002	.0003
14									.0001	.0001

m =	4.1	4.2	4.3	4.4	4.5	4.6	4.7	4.8	4.9	5.0
r = 0	1.0000	1.0000	1.0000	1.0000	1.0000	1.0000	1.0000	1.0000	1.0000	1.0000
1	.9834	.9850	.9864	.9877	.9889	.9899	.9909	.9918	.9926	.9933
2	.9155	.9220	.9281	.9337	.9389	.9437	.9482	.9523	.9561	.9596
3	.7762	.7898	.8026	.8149	.8264	.8374	.8477	.8575	.8667	.8753
4	.5858	.6046	.6228	.6406	.6577	.6743	.6903	.7058	.7207	.7350
5	.3907	.4102	.4296	.4488	.4679	.4868	.5054	.5237	.5418	.5595
6	.2307	.2469	.2633	.2801	.2971	.3142	.3316	.3490	.3665	.3840
7	.1214	.1325	.1442	.1564	.1689	.1820	.1954	.2092	.2233	.2378
8	.0573	.0639	.0710	.0786	.0866	.0951	.1040	.1133	.1231	.1334
9	.0245	.0279	.0317	.0358	.0403	.0451	.0503	.0558	.0618	.0681
10	.0095	.0111	.0129	.0149	.0171	.0195	.0222	.0251	.0283	.0318
11	.0034	.0041	.0048	.0057	.0067	.0078	.0090	.0104	.0120	.0137
12	.0011	.0014	.0017	.0020	.0024	.0029	.0034	.0040	.0047	.0055
13	.0003	.0004	.0005	.0007	.0008	.0010	.0012	.0014	.0017	.0020
14	.0001	.0001	.0002	.0002	.0003	.0003	.0004	.0005	.0006	.0007
15				.0001	.0001	.0001	.0001	.0001	.0002	.0002
16									.0001	.0001

m =	5.2	5.4	5.6	5.8	6.0	6.2	6.4	6.6	6.8	7.0
r = 0	1.0000	1.0000	1.0000	1.0000	1.0000	1.0000	1.0000	1.0000	1.0000	1.0000
1	.9945	.9955	.9963	.9970	.9975	.9980	.9983	.9986	.9989	.9991
2	.9658	.9711	.9756	.9794	.9826	.9854	.9877	.9897	.9913	.9927
3	.8912	.9052	.9176	.9285	.9380	.9464	.9537	.9600	.9656	.9704
4	.7619	.7867	.8094	.8300	.8488	.8658	.8811	.8948	.9072	.9182
5	.5939	.6267	.6579	.6873	.7149	.7408	.7649	.7873	.8080	.8270
6	.4191	.4539	.4881	.5217	.5543	.5859	.6163	.6453	.6730	.6993
7	.2676	.2983	.3297	.3616	.3937	.4258	.4577	.4892	.5201	.5503
8	.1551	.1783	.2030	.2290	.2560	.2840	.3127	.3419	.3715	.4013
9	.0819	.0974	.1143	.1328	.1528	.1741	.1967	.2204	.2452	.2709
10	.0397	.0488	.0591	.0708	.0839	.0984	.1142	.1314	.1498	.1695
11	.0177	.0225	.0282	.0349	.0426	.0514	.0614	.0726	.0849	.0985
12	.0073	.0096	.0125	.0160	.0201	.0250	.0307	.0373	.0448	.0534
13	.0028	.0038	.0051	.0068	.0088	.0113	.0143	.0179	.0221	.0270
14	.0010	.0014	.0020	.0027	.0036	.0048	.0063	.0080	.0102	.0128
15	.0003	.0005	.0007	.0010	.0014	.0019	.0026	.0034	.0044	.0057
16	.0001	.0002	.0002	.0004	.0005	.0007	.0010	.0014	.0018	.0024
17		.0001	.0001	.0001	.0002	.0003	.0004	.0005	.0007	.0010
18					.0001	.0001	.0001	.0002	.0003	.0004
19								.0001	.0001	.0001

$\lambda =$	7.2	7.4	7.6	7.8	8.0	8.2	8.4	8.6	8.8	9.0
= 0	1.0000	1.0000	1.0000	1.0000	1.0000	1.0000	1.0000	1.0000	1.0000	1.0000
1	.9993	.9994	.9995	.9996	.9997	.9997	.9998	.9998	.9998	.9999
2	.9939	.9949	.9957	.9964	.9970	.9975	.9979	.9982	.9985	.9988
3	.9745	.9781	.9812	.9839	.9862	.9882	.9900	.9914	.9927	.9938
4	.9281	.9368	.9446	.9515	.9576	.9630	.9677	.9719	.9756	.9788
5	.8445	.8605	.8751	.8883	.9004	.9113	.9211	.9299	.9379	.9450
6	.7241	.7474	.7693	.7897	.8088	.8264	.8427	.8578	.8716	.8843
7	.5796	.6080	.6354	.6616	.6866	.7104	.7330	.7543	.7744	.7932
8	.4311	.4607	.4900	.5188	.5470	.5746	.6013	.6272	.6522	.6761
9	.2973	.3243	.3518	.3796	.4075	.4353	.4631	.4906	.5177	.5443
10	.1904	.2123	.2351	.2589	.2834	.3085	.3341	.3600	.3863	.4126
11	.1133	.1293	.1465	.1648	.1841	.2045	.2257	.2478	.2706	.2940
12	.0629	.0735	.0852	.0980	.1119	.1269	.1429	.1600	.1780	.1970
13	.0327	.0391	.0464	.0546	.0638	.0739	.0850	.0971	.1102	.1242
14	.0159	.0195	.0238	.0286	.0342	.0405	.0476	.0555	.0642	.0739
15	.0073	.0092	.0114	.0141	.0173	.0209	.0251	.0299	.0353	.0415
16	.0031	.0041	.0052	.0066	.0082	.0102	.0125	.0152	.0184	.0220
17	.0013	.0017	.0022	.0029	.0037	.0047	.0059	.0074	.0091	.0111
18	.0005	.0007	.0009	.0012	.0016	.0021	.0027	.0034	.0043	.0053
19	.0002	.0003	.0004	.0005	.0006	.0009	.0011	.0015	.0019	.0024
20	.0001	.0001	.0001	.0002	.0003	.0003	.0005	.0006	.0008	.0011
21				.0001	.0001	.0001	.0002	.0002	.0003	.0004
22							.0001	.0001	.0001	.0002
23										.0001

$\lambda =$	9.2	9.4	9.6	9.8	10.0	11.0	12.0	13.0	14.0	15.0
= 0	1.0000	1.0000	1.0000	1.0000	1.0000	1.0000	1.0000	1.0000	1.0000	1.0000
1	.9999	.9999	.9999	.9999	1.0000	1.0000	1.0000	1.0000	1.0000	1.0000
2	.9990	.9991	.9993	.9994	.9995	.9998	.9999	1.0000	1.0000	1.0000
3	.9947	.9955	.9962	.9967	.9972	.9988	.9995	.9998	.9999	1.0000
4	.9816	.9840	.9862	.9880	.9897	.9951	.9977	.9990	.9995	.9998
5	.9514	.9571	.9622	.9667	.9707	.9849	.9924	.9963	.9982	.9991
6	.8959	.9065	.9162	.9250	.9329	.9625	.9797	.9893	.9945	.9972
7	.8108	.8273	.8426	.8567	.8699	.9214	.9542	.9741	.9858	.9924
8	.6990	.7208	.7416	.7612	.7798	.8568	.9105	.9460	.9684	.9820
9	.5704	.5958	.6204	.6442	.6672	.7680	.8450	.9002	.9379	.9626
10	.4389	.4651	.4911	.5168	.5421	.6595	.7576	.8342	.8906	.9301
11	.3180	.3424	.3671	.3920	.4170	.5401	.6528	.7483	.8243	.8815
12	.2168	.2374	.2588	.2807	.3032	.4207	.5384	.6468	.7400	.8152
13	.1393	.1552	.1721	.1899	.2084	.3113	.4240	.5369	.6415	.7324
14	.0844	.0958	.1081	.1214	.1355	.2187	.3185	.4270	.5356	.6368
15	.0483	.0559	.0643	.0735	.0835	.1460	.2280	.3249	.4296	.5343
16	.0262	.0309	.0362	.0421	.0487	.0926	.1556	.2364	.3306	.4319
17	.0135	.0162	.0194	.0230	.0270	.0559	.1013	.1645	.2441	.3359
18	.0066	.0081	.0098	.0119	.0143	.0322	.0630	.1095	.1728	.2511
19	.0031	.0038	.0048	.0059	.0072	.0177	.0374	.0698	.1174	.1805
20	.0014	.0017	.0022	.0028	.0035	.0093	.0213	.0427	.0765	.1248
21	.0006	.0008	.0010	.0012	.0016	.0047	.0116	.0250	.0479	.0830
22	.0002	.0003	.0004	.0005	.0007	.0023	.0061	.0141	.0288	.0531
23	.0001	.0001	.0002	.0002	.0003	.0010	.0030	.0076	.0167	.0327
24			.0001	.0001	.0001	.0005	.0015	.0040	.0093	.0195
25						.0002	.0007	.0020	.0050	.0112
26						.0001	.0003	.0010	.0026	.0062
27							.0001	.0005	.0013	.0033
28							.0001	.0002	.0006	.0017
29								.0001	.0003	.0009
30									.0001	.0004
31									.0001	.0002
32										.0001

Table 1 continued Cumulative Poisson Probabilities

$m =$	16.0	17.0	18.0	19.0	20.0	21.0	22.0	23.0	24.0	25.0
$r =$ 0	1.0000	1.0000	1.0000	1.0000	1.0000	1.0000	1.0000	1.0000	1.0000	1.0000
1	1.0000	1.0000	1.0000	1.0000	1.0000	1.0000	1.0000	1.0000	1.0000	1.0000
2	1.0000	1.0000	1.0000	1.0000	1.0000	1.0000	1.0000	1.0000	1.0000	1.0000
3	1.0000	1.0000	1.0000	1.0000	1.0000	1.0000	1.0000	1.0000	1.0000	1.0000
4	.9999	1.0000	1.0000	1.0000	1.0000	1.0000	1.0000	1.0000	1.0000	1.0000
5	.9996	.9998	.9999	1.0000	1.0000	1.0000	1.0000	1.0000	1.0000	1.0000
6	.9986	.9993	.9997	.9998	.9999	1.0000	1.0000	1.0000	1.0000	1.0000
7	.9960	.9979	.9990	.9995	.9997	.9999	.9999	1.0000	1.0000	1.0000
8	.9900	.9946	.9971	.9985	.9992	.9996	.9998	.9999	1.0000	1.0000
9	.9780	.9874	.9929	.9961	.9979	.9989	.9994	.9997	.9998	.9999
10	.9567	.9739	.9846	.9911	.9950	.9972	.9985	.9992	.9996	.9998
11	.9226	.9509	.9696	.9817	.9892	.9937	.9965	.9980	.9989	.9994
12	.8730	.9153	.9451	.9653	.9786	.9871	.9924	.9956	.9975	.9986
13	.8069	.8650	.9083	.9394	.9610	.9755	.9849	.9909	.9946	.9969
14	.7255	.7991	.8574	.9016	.9339	.9566	.9722	.9826	.9893	.9935
15	.6325	.7192	.7919	.8503	.8951	.9284	.9523	.9689	.9802	.9876
16	.5333	.6285	.7133	.7852	.8435	.8889	.9231	.9480	.9656	.9777
17	.4340	.5323	.6249	.7080	.7789	.8371	.8830	.9179	.9437	.9623
18	.3407	.4360	.5314	.6216	.7030	.7730	.8310	.8772	.9129	.9395
19	.2577	.3450	.4378	.5305	.6186	.6983	.7675	.8252	.8717	.9080
20	.1878	.2637	.3491	.4394	.5297	.6157	.6940	.7623	.8197	.8664
21	.1318	.1945	.2693	.3528	.4409	.5290	.6131	.6899	.7574	.8145
22	.0892	.1385	.2009	.2745	.3563	.4423	.5284	.6106	.6861	.7527
23	.0582	.0953	.1449	.2069	.2794	.3595	.4436	.5277	.6083	.6825
24	.0367	.0633	.1011	.1510	.2125	.2840	.3626	.4449	.5272	.6061

Table 1 continued Cumulative Poisson Probabilities

$m =$	16.0	17.0	18.0	19.0	20.0	21.0	22.0	23.0	24.0	25.0
$r = 25$	.0223	.0406	.0683	.1067	.1568	.2178	.2883	.3654	.4460	.5266
26	.0131	.0252	.0446	.0731	.1122	.1623	.2229	.2923	.3681	.4471
27	.0075	.0152	.0282	.0486	.0779	.1174	.1676	.2277	.2962	.3706
28	.0041	.0088	.0173	.0313	.0525	.0825	.1225	.1726	.2323	.2998
29	.0022	.0050	.0103	.0195	.0343	.0564	.0871	.1274	.1775	.2366
30	.0011	.0027	.0059	.0118	.0218	.0374	.0602	.0915	.1321	.1821
31	.0006	.0014	.0033	.0070	.0135	.0242	.0405	.0640	.0958	.1367
32	.0003	.0007	.0018	.0040	.0081	.0152	.0265	.0436	.0678	.1001
33	.0001	.0004	.0010	.0022	.0047	.0093	.0169	.0289	.0467	.0715
34	.0001	.0002	.0005	.0012	.0027	.0055	.0105	.0187	.0314	.0498
35		.0001	.0002	.0006	.0015	.0032	.0064	.0118	.0206	.0338
36			.0001	.0003	.0008	.0018	.0038	.0073	.0132	.0225
37			.0001	.0002	.0004	.0010	.0022	.0044	.0082	.0146
38				.0001	.0002	.0005	.0012	.0026	.0050	.0092
39					.0001	.0003	.0007	.0015	.0030	.0057
40					.0001	.0001	.0004	.0008	.0017	.0034
41						.0001	.0002	.0004	.0010	.0020
42							.0001	.0002	.0005	.0012
43								.0001	.0003	.0007
44								.0001	.0002	.0004
45									.0001	.0002
46										.0001

Table 1 continued Cumulative Poisson Probabilities

m =	26.0	27.0	28.0	29.0	30.0	32.0	34.0	36.0	38.0	40.0
r = 9	1.0000	1.0000	1.0000	1.0000	1.0000	1.0000	1.0000	1.0000	1.0000	1.0000
10	.9999	.9999	1.0000	1.0000	1.0000	1.0000	1.0000	1.0000	1.0000	1.0000
11	.9997	.9998	.9999	1.0000	1.0000	1.0000	1.0000	1.0000	1.0000	1.0000
12	.9992	.9996	.9999	.9999	.9999	1.0000	1.0000	1.0000	1.0000	1.0000
13	.9982	.9990	.9994	.9997	.9998	1.0000	1.0000	1.0000	1.0000	1.0000
14	.9962	.9978	.9987	.9993	.9996	.9999	1.0000	1.0000	1.0000	1.0000
15	.9924	.9954	.9973	.9984	.9991	.9997	.9999	1.0000	1.0000	1.0000
16	.9858	.9912	.9946	.9967	.9981	.9993	.9998	.9999	1.0000	1.0000
17	.9752	.9840	.9899	.9937	.9961	.9986	.9995	.9998	1.0000	1.0000
18	.9580	.9726	.9821	.9885	.9927	.9972	.9990	.9997	.9999	1.0000
19	.9354	.9555	.9700	.9801	.9871	.9948	.9980	.9993	.9998	.9999
20	.9032	.9313	.9522	.9674	.9781	.9907	.9963	.9986	.9995	.9998
21	.8613	.8985	.9273	.9489	.9647	.9841	.9932	.9973	.9990	.9996
22	.8095	.8564	.8940	.9233	.9456	.9740	.9884	.9951	.9981	.9993
23	.7483	.8048	.8517	.8896	.9194	.9594	.9809	.9915	.9965	.9986
24	.6791	.7441	.8002	.8471	.8854	.9390	.9698	.9859	.9938	.9974
25	.6041	.6758	.7401	.7958	.8428	.9119	.9540	.9776	.9897	.9955
26	.5261	.6021	.6728	.7363	.7916	.8772	.9326	.9655	.9834	.9924
27	.4481	.5256	.6003	.6699	.7327	.8344	.9047	.9487	.9741	.9877
28	.3730	.4491	.5251	.5986	.6671	.7838	.8694	.9264	.9611	.9807
29	.3033	.3753	.4500	.5247	.5969	.7259	.8267	.8977	.9435	.9706
30	.2407	.3065	.3774	.4508	.5243	.6620	.7765	.8621	.9204	.9568
31	.1866	.2447	.3097	.3794	.4516	.5939	.7196	.8194	.8911	.9383
32	.1411	.1908	.2485	.3126	.3814	.5235	.6573	.7697	.8552	.9145
33	.1042	.1454	.1949	.2521	.3155	.4532	.5911	.7139	.8125	.8847
34	.0751	.1082	.1495	.1989	.2556	.3850	.5228	.6530	.7635	.8486
35	.0528	.0787	.1121	.1535	.2027	.3208	.4546	.5885	.7086	.8061
36	.0363	.0559	.0822	.1159	.1574	.2621	.3883	.5222	.6490	.7576
37	.0244	.0388	.0589	.0856	.1196	.2099	.3256	.4558	.5862	.7037
38	.0160	.0263	.0413	.0619	.0890	.1648	.2681	.3913	.5216	.6453
39	.0103	.0175	.0283	.0438	.0648	.1268	.2166	.3301	.4570	.5840

Table 1 continued Cumulative Poisson Probabilities

$m =$	26.0	27.0	28.0	29.0	30.0	32.0	34.0	36.0	38.0	40.0
$r =$ 40	.0064	.0113	.0190	.0303	.0463	.0956	.1717	.2737	.3941	.5210
41	.0039	.0072	.0125	.0205	.0323	.0707	.1336	.2229	.3343	.4581
42	.0024	.0045	.0080	.0136	.0221	.0512	.1019	.1783	.2789	.3967
43	.0014	.0027	.0050	.0089	.0148	.0364	.0763	.1401	.2288	.3382
44	.0008	.0016	.0031	.0056	.0097	.0253	.0561	.1081	.1845	.2838
45	.0004	.0009	.0019	.0035	.0063	.0173	.0404	.0819	.1462	.2343
46	.0002	.0005	.0011	.0022	.0040	.0116	.0286	.0609	.1139	.1903
47	.0001	.0003	.0006	.0013	.0025	.0076	.0199	.0445	.0872	.1521
48	.0001	.0002	.0004	.0008	.0015	.0049	.0136	.0320	.0657	.1196
49		.0001	.0002	.0004	.0009	.0031	.0091	.0225	.0486	.0925
50		.0001	.0001	.0002	.0005	.0019	.0060	.0156	.0353	.0703
51			.0001	.0001	.0003	.0012	.0039	.0106	.0253	.0526
52				.0001	.0002	.0007	.0024	.0071	.0178	.0387
53					.0001	.0004	.0015	.0047	.0123	.0281
54					.0001	.0002	.0009	.0030	.0084	.0200
55						.0001	.0006	.0019	.0056	.0140
56						.0001	.0003	.0012	.0037	.0097
57							.0002	.0007	.0024	.0066
58							.0001	.0005	.0015	.0044
59							.0001	.0003	.0010	.0029
60								.0002	.0006	.0019
61								.0001	.0004	.0012
62								.0001	.0002	.0008
63									.0001	.0005
64									.0001	.0003
65										.0002
66										.0001
67										.0001

For values of m greater than 30, use the table of areas under the normal curve (Table 2) to obtain approximate Poisson probabilities, putting $\mu = m$ and $\sigma = \sqrt{m}$.

Table 2 Areas in Tail of the Normal Distribution

The function tabulated is $1 - \Phi(u)$ where $\Phi(u)$ is the cumulative distribution function of a standardised normal variable u. Thus

$$1 - \Phi(u) = \frac{1}{\sqrt{2\pi}} \int_u^\infty e^{-x^2/2} \, dx$$

is the probability that a standardised normal variable selected at random will be greater than a value of u $\left(= \dfrac{x-\mu}{\sigma}\right)$

$\dfrac{(x-\mu)}{\sigma}$	.00	.01	.02	.03	.04	.05	.06	.07	.08	.09
0.0	.5000	.4960	.4920	.4880	.4840	.4801	.4761	.4721	.4681	.4641
0.1	.4602	.4562	.4522	.4483	.4443	.4404	.4364	.4325	.4286	.4247
0.2	.4207	.4168	.4129	.4090	.4052	.4013	.3974	.3936	.3897	.3859
0.3	.3821	.3783	.3745	.3707	.3669	.3632	.3594	.3557	.3520	.3483
0.4	.3446	.3409	.3372	.3336	.3300	.3264	.3228	.3192	.3156	.3121
0.5	.3085	.3050	.3015	.2981	.2946	.2912	.2877	.2843	.2810	.2776
0.6	.2743	.2709	.2676	.2643	.2611	.2578	.2546	.2514	.2483	.2451
0.7	.2420	.2389	.2358	.2327	.2296	.2266	.2236	.2206	.2177	.2148
0.8	.2119	.2090	.2061	.2033	.2005	.1977	.1949	.1922	.1894	.1867
0.9	.1841	.1814	.1788	.1762	.1736	.1711	.1685	.1660	.1635	.1611
1.0	.1587	.1562	.1539	.1515	.1492	.1469	.1446	.1423	.1401	.1379
1.1	.1357	.1335	.1314	.1292	.1271	.1251	.1230	.1210	.1190	.1170
1.2	.1151	.1131	.1112	.1093	.1075	.1056	.1038	.1020	.1003	.0985
1.3	.0968	.0951	.0934	.0918	.0901	.0885	.0869	.0853	.0838	.0823
1.4	.0808	.0793	.0778	.0764	.0749	.0735	.0721	.0708	.0694	.0681

Table 2 continued Areas in Tail of the Normal Distribution

	.00	.01	.02	.03	.04	.05	.06	.07	.08	.09
1.5	.0668	.0655	.0643	.0630	.0618	.0606	.0594	.0582	.0571	.0559
1.6	.0548	.0537	.0526	.0516	.0505	.0495	.0485	.0475	.0465	.0455
1.7	.0446	.0436	.0427	.0418	.0409	.0401	.0392	.0384	.0375	.0367
1.8	.0359	.0351	.0344	.0336	.0329	.0322	.0314	.0307	.0301	.0294
1.9	.0287	.0281	.0274	.0268	.0262	.0256	.0250	.0244	.0239	.0233
2.0	.02275	.02222	.02169	.02118	.02068	.02018	.01970	.01923	.01876	.01831
2.1	.01786	.01743	.01700	.01659	.01618	.01578	.01539	.01500	.01463	.01426
2.2	.01390	.01355	.01321	.01287	.01255	.01222	.01191	.01160	.01130	.01101
2.3	.01072	.01044	.01017	.00990	.00964	.00939	.00914	.00889	.00866	.00842
2.4	.00820	.00798	.00776	.00755	.00734	.00714	.00695	.00676	.00657	.00639
2.5	.00621	.00604	.00587	.00570	.00554	.00539	.00523	.00508	.00494	.00480
2.6	.00466	.00453	.00440	.00427	.00415	.00402	.00391	.00379	.00368	.00357
2.7	.00347	.00336	.00326	.00317	.00307	.00298	.00289	.00280	.00272	.00264
2.8	.00256	.00248	.00240	.00233	.00226	.00219	.00212	.00205	.00199	.00193
2.9	.00187	.00181	.00175	.00169	.00164	.00159	.00154	.00149	.00144	.00139
3.0	.00135									
3.1	.00097									
3.2	.00069									
3.3	.00048									
3.4	.00034									
3.5	.00023									
3.6	.00016									
3.7	.00011									
3.8	.00007									
3.9	.00005									
4.0	.00003									

Table 3 Percentage Points of the χ^2 Distribution

Table of $\chi^2_{\alpha;\,\nu}$ – the 100 α percentage point of the χ^2 distribution for ν degrees of freedom

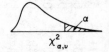

$\alpha =$	.995	.99	.98	.975	.95	.90	.80	.75	.70
$\nu = 1$	.0⁴393	.0³157	.0³628	.0³982	.00393	.0158	.0642	.102	.148
2	.0100	.0201	.0404	.0506	.103	.211	.446	.575	.713
3	.0717	.115	.185	.216	.352	.584	1.005	1.213	1.424
4	.207	.297	.429	.484	.711	1.064	1.649	1.923	2.195
5	.412	.554	.752	.831	1.145	1.610	2.343	2.675	3.000
6	.676	.872	1.134	1.237	1.635	2.204	3.070	3.455	3.828
7	.989	1.239	1.564	1.690	2.167	2.833	3.822	4.255	4.671
8	1.344	1.646	2.032	2.180	2.733	3.490	4.594	5.071	5.527
9	1.735	2.088	2.532	2.700	3.325	4.168	5.380	5.899	6.393
10	2.156	2.558	3.059	3.247	3.940	4.865	6.179	6.737	7.267
11	2.603	3.053	3.609	3.816	4.575	5.578	6.989	7.584	8.148
12	3.074	3.571	4.178	4.404	5.226	6.304	7.807	8.438	9.034
13	3.565	4.107	4.765	5.009	5.892	7.042	8.634	9.299	9.926
14	4.075	4.660	5.368	5.629	6.571	7.790	9.467	10.165	10.821
15	4.601	5.229	5.985	6.262	7.261	8.547	10.307	11.036	11.721
16	5.142	5.812	6.614	6.908	7.962	9.312	11.152	11.912	12.624
17	5.697	6.408	7.255	7.564	8.672	10.085	12.002	12.792	13.531
18	6.265	7.015	7.906	8.231	9.390	10.865	12.857	13.675	14.440
19	6.844	7.633	8.567	8.907	10.117	11.651	13.716	14.562	15.352
20	7.434	8.260	9.237	9.591	10.851	12.443	14.578	15.452	16.266
21	8.034	8.897	9.915	10.283	11.591	13.240	15.445	16.344	17.182
22	8.643	9.542	10.600	10.982	12.338	14.041	16.314	17.240	18.101
23	9.260	10.196	11.293	11.688	13.091	14.848	17.187	18.137	19.021
24	9.886	10.856	11.992	12.401	13.848	15.659	18.062	19.037	19.943
25	10.520	11.524	12.697	13.120	14.611	16.473	18.940	19.939	20.867
26	11.160	12.198	13.409	13.844	15.379	17.292	19.820	20.843	21.792
27	11.808	12.879	14.125	14.573	16.151	18.114	20.703	21.749	22.719
28	12.461	13.565	14.847	15.308	16.928	18.939	21.588	22.657	23.647
29	13.121	14.256	15.574	16.047	17.708	19.768	22.475	23.567	24.577
30	13.787	14.953	16.306	16.791	18.493	20.599	23.364	24.478	25.508
40	20.706	22.164	23.838	24.433	26.509	29.051	32.345	33.660	34.872
50	27.991	29.707	31.664	32.357	34.764	37.689	41.449	42.942	44.313
60	35.535	37.485	39.699	40.482	43.188	46.459	50.641	52.294	53.809
70	43.275	45.442	47.893	48.758	51.739	55.329	59.898	61.698	63.346
80	51.171	53.539	56.213	57.153	60.391	64.278	69.207	71.145	72.915
90	59.196	61.754	64.634	65.646	69.126	73.291	78.558	80.625	82.511
100	67.327	70.065	73.142	74.222	77.929	82.358	87.945	90.133	92.129

For values of $\nu > 30$, approximate values for χ^2 may be obtained from the expression
$$\nu \left[1 - \frac{2}{9\nu} \pm \frac{x}{\sigma} \sqrt{\frac{2}{9\nu}} \right]^3$$
, where x/σ is the normal deviate cutting off the corresponding tails of a normal distribution. If x/σ is taken at the 0.02 level, so that 0.01 of the normal distribution is in each tail, the expression yields χ^2 at the 0.99 and 0.01 points. For very large values of ν, it

Table 3 continued Percentage Points of the χ^2 Distribution

.50	.30	.25	.20	.10	.05	.025	.02	.01	.005	.001	= α
.455	1.074	1.323	1.642	2.706	3.841	5.024	5.412	6.635	7.879	10.827	ν = 1
1.386	2.408	2.773	3.219	4.605	5.991	7.378	7.824	9.210	10.597	13.815	2
2.366	3.665	4.108	4.642	6.251	7.815	9.348	9.837	11.345	12.838	16.268	3
3.357	4.878	5.385	5.989	7.779	9.488	11.143	11.668	13.277	14.860	18.465	4
4.351	6.064	6.626	7.289	9.236	11.070	12.832	13.388	15.086	16.750	20.517	5
5.348	7.231	7.841	8.558	10.645	12.592	14.449	15.033	16.812	18.548	22.457	6
6.346	8.383	9.037	9.803	12.017	14.067	16.013	16.622	18.475	20.278	24.322	7
7.344	9.524	10.219	11.030	13.362	15.507	17.535	18.168	20.090	21.955	26.125	8
8.343	10.656	11.389	12.242	14.684	16.919	19.023	19.679	21.666	23.589	27.877	9
9.342	11.781	12.549	13.442	15.987	18.307	20.483	21.161	23.209	25.188	29.588	10
10.341	12.899	13.701	14.631	17.275	19.675	21.920	22.618	24.725	26.757	31.264	11
11.340	14.011	14.845	15.812	18.549	21.026	23.337	24.054	26.217	28.300	32.909	12
12.340	15.119	15.984	16.985	19.812	22.362	24.736	25.472	27.688	29.819	34.528	13
13.339	16.222	17.117	18.151	21.064	23.685	26.119	26.873	29.141	31.319	36.123	14
14.339	17.322	18.245	19.311	22.307	24.996	27.488	28.259	30.578	32.801	37.697	15
15.338	18.418	19.369	20.465	23.542	26.296	28.845	29.633	32.000	34.267	39.252	16
16.338	19.511	20.489	21.615	24.769	27.587	30.191	30.995	33.409	35.718	40.790	17
17.338	20.601	21.605	22.760	25.989	28.869	31.526	32.346	34.805	37.156	42.312	18
18.338	21.689	22.718	23.900	27.204	30.144	32.852	33.687	36.191	38.582	43.820	19
19.337	22.775	23.828	25.038	28.412	31.410	34.170	35.020	37.566	39.997	45.315	20
20.337	23.858	24.935	26.171	29.615	32.671	35.479	36.343	38.932	41.401	46.797	21
21.337	24.939	26.039	27.301	30.813	33.924	36.781	37.659	40.289	42.796	48.268	22
22.337	26.018	27.141	28.429	32.007	35.172	38.076	38.968	41.638	44.181	49.728	23
23.337	27.096	28.241	29.553	33.196	36.415	39.364	40.270	42.980	45.558	51.179	24
24.337	28.172	29.339	30.675	34.382	37.652	40.646	41.566	44.314	46.928	52.620	25
25.336	29.246	30.434	31.795	35.563	38.885	41.923	42.856	45.642	48.290	54.052	26
26.336	30.319	31.528	32.912	36.741	40.113	43.194	44.140	46.963	49.645	55.476	27
27.336	31.391	32.620	34.027	37.916	41.337	44.461	45.419	48.278	50.993	56.893	28
28.336	32.461	33.711	35.139	39.087	42.557	45.722	46.693	49.588	52.336	58.302	29
29.336	33.530	34.800	36.250	40.256	43.773	46.979	47.962	50.892	53.672	59.703	30
39.335	44.165	45.616	47.269	51.805	55.759	59.342	60.436	63.691	66.766	73.402	40
49.335	54.723	56.334	58.164	63.167	67.505	71.420	72.613	76.154	79.490	86.661	50
59.335	65.227	66.981	68.972	74.397	79.082	83.298	84.580	88.379	91.952	99.607	60
69.334	75.689	77.577	79.715	85.527	90.531	95.023	96.388	100.425	104.215	112.317	70
79.334	86.120	88.130	90.405	96.578	101.880	106.629	108.069	112.329	116.321	124.839	80
89.334	96.524	98.650	101.054	107.565	113.145	118.136	119.648	124.116	128.299	137.208	90
99.334	106.906	109.141	111.667	118.498	124.342	129.561	131.142	135.807	140.170	149.449	100

is sufficiently accurate to compute $\sqrt{(2\chi^2)}$, the distribution of which is approximately normal around a mean of $\sqrt{2\nu - 1}$, and with a standard deviation of 1. This table is taken by consent from 'Statistical Tables for Biological, Agricultural, and Medical Research', by R. A. Fisher and F. Yates, published by Oliver and Boyd, Edinburgh, and from Table 8 of 'Biometrika Tables for Statisticians, Vol. 1, by permission of the Biometrika Trustees.

Table 4 Control Chart Limits for Sample Average ($\overline{X}$)

To obtain the limits $\begin{cases}\text{multiply } \sigma \text{ by the appropriate value of } A_{0.025} \text{ and } A_{0.001} \text{ or} \\ \text{multiply } w \text{ by the appropriate value of } A'_{0.025} \text{ and } A'_{0.001}\end{cases}$
then add to and subtract from the average value ($\overline{x}$)

No. in sample (n)	For inner limits ($A_{0.025}$)	For outer limits ($A_{0.001}$)	For inner limits ($A'_{0.025}$)	For outer limits ($A'_{0.001}$)
2	1.386	2.185	1.229	1.937
3	1.132	1.784	0.668	1.054
4	0.980	1.545	0.476	0.750
5	0.876	1.382	0.377	0.594
6	0.800	1.262	0.316	0.498
7	0.741	1.168	0.274	0.432
8	0.693	1.092	0.244	0.384
9	0.653	1.030	0.220	0.347
10	0.620	0.977	0.202	0.317
11	0.591	0.932	0.186	0.294
12	0.566	0.892	0.174	0.274
13	0.544	0.857		

Table 4 continued Control Chart Limits for Sample Average ($\overline{X}$)

No. in sample (n)	For inner limits ($A_{0.025}$)	For outer limits ($A_{0.001}$)	
14	0.524	0.826	Samples containing more than 12 individuals should not be used when utilising the range in the results.
15	0.506	0.798	
16	0.490	0.773	
17	0.475	0.750	
18	0.462	0.728	
19	0.450	0.709	These factors should only be used when it is not necessary to calculate s for the samples and when sufficient test data are available to make an accurate estimate of σ from $\overline{w}$
20	0.438	0.691	
21	0.428	0.674	
22	0.418	0.659	
23	0.409	0.644	
24	0.400	0.631	
25	0.392	0.618	
26	0.384	0.606	
27	0.377	0.595	
28	0.370	0.584	
29	0.364	0.574	
30	0.358	0.564	

This extract from B. S. 600 R: 1942 'Quality Control Charts' is reproduced by permission of the British Standards Institution, 2 Park Street, London, W. 1. Although B. S. 600 R is now withdrawn the table appears in an abridged form in B. S. 2564: 1955 'Control Technique'.

Table 5 Control Chart Limits for Sample Range Using $\bar{w}$

To obtain the limits, multiply $\bar{w}$ by the appropriate value of D'.

No. in sample (n)	For lower limits $D'_{0.999}$	$D'_{0.975}$	For upper limits $D'_{0.025}$	$D'_{0.001}$
2	0.00	0.04	2.81	4.12
3	0.04	0.18	2.17	2.98
4	0.10	0.29	1.93	2.57
5	0.16	0.37	1.81	2.34
6	0.21	0.42	1.72	2.21
7	0.26	0.46	1.66	2.11
8	0.29	0.50	1.62	2.04
9	0.32	0.52	1.58	1.99
10	0.35	0.54	1.56	1.93
11	0.38	0.56	1.53	1.91
12	0.40	0.58	1.51	1.87

This extract from B.S. 600 R: 1942 'Quality Control Charts' is reproduced by permission of the British Standards Institution, 2 Park Street, London W.1. Although B.S. 600R is now withdrawn the table appears in an abridged form in B.S. 2564: 1955 'Control Chart Technique'.

Table 6 Control Chart Limits for Sample Range Using σ

To obtain the limits, multiply σ by the appropriate value of D.
To obtain the average value $\bar{w}$, multiply σ by the appropriate value of d_n.

No. in sample (n)	For lower limits Outer $(D_{0.999})$	Inner $(D_{0.975})$	For upper limits Inner $(D_{0.025})$	Outer $(D_{0.001})$	For average value of w, $(\bar{w})$ d_n
2	0.00	0.04	3.17	4.65	1.128
3	0.06	0.30	3.68	5.05	1.693
4	0.20	0.59	3.98	5.30	2.059
5	0.37	0.85	4.20	5.45	2.326
6	0.54	1.06	4.36	5.60	2.534
7	0.69	1.25	4.49	5.70	2.704
8	0.83	1.41	4.61	5.80	2.847
9	0.96	1.55	4.70	5.90	2.970
10	1.08	1.67	4.79	5.95	3.078
11	1.20	1.78	4.86	6.05	3.173
12	1.30	1.88	4.92	6.10	3.258

This extract from the withdrawn standard B.S. 600R: 1942 'Quality Control Charts' is reproduced by permission of the British Standards Institution, 2 Park Street, London, W.1.

Table 7 American Type Shewhart Control Charts (3 σ limits)

Sample size (n)	Multiplying factors		
	A_2	D_3	D_4
2	1.880	0.0	3.268
3	1.023	0.0	2.574
4	0.729	0.0	2.282
5	0.577	0.0	2.114
6	0.483	0.0	2.004
7	0.419	0.076	1.924
8	0.373	0.136	1.864
9	0.337	0.184	1.816
10	0.308	0.223	1.777
11	0.285	0.256	1.744
12	0.266	0.284	1.717

Control Limits

Process average chart
Upper control limit = $\bar{X} + A_2 \bar{w}$
Lower control limit = $\bar{X} - A_2 \bar{w}$

Range chart
Upper control limit = $D_4 \bar{w}$
Lower control limit = $D_3 \bar{w}$

Table 8 Nomogram for Designing CuSum Control Schemes

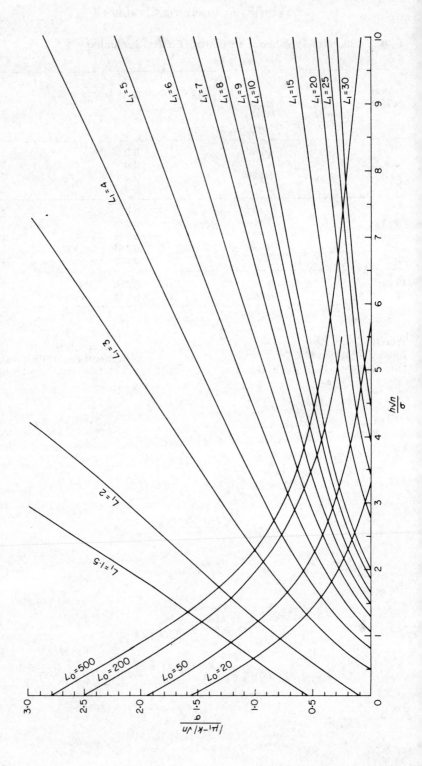

Table 9 Design of Attribute CuSum Schemes. Parameters for the Design of Attribute CuSum Control Systems Given $L_0 = 500$ for Range of Values of m_1 up to $m_1 = 10$

Average No. of defects/sample at R.Q.L. (m_2) and ratio $R = m_2/m_1$ for values of average run length to detection L_1 up to 10.

Average defects/sample at A.Q.L. (m_1)	Decision interval (h)	Reference value (k)	$L_1=2$ m_2	$L_1=2$ R	$L_1=4$ m_2	$L_1=4$ R	$L_1=5$ m_2	$L_1=5$ R	$L_1=6$ m_2	$L_1=6$ R	$L_1=8$ m_2	$L_1=8$ R	$L_1=9$ m_2	$L_1=9$ R	$L_1=10$ m_2	$L_1=10$ R
0.22	2	1	2.40	10.9	1.48	6.7	1.30	5.9	1.16	5.3	1.01	4.6	0.96	4.4	0.91	4.1
0.39	3	1	3.00	7.7	1.83	4.7	1.61	4.1	1.46	3.7	1.28	3.3	1.21	3.1	1.16	3.0
0.51	2	2	3.40	6.7	2.30	4.5	2.10	4.1	1.94	3.8	1.74	3.4	1.66	3.3	1.60	3.1
0.62	5	1	4.39	7.1	2.45	4.0	2.11	3.4	1.90	3.1	1.63	2.6	1.55	2.5	1.48	2.4
0.69	6	1	5.06	7.3	2.75	4.0	2.35	3.4	2.10	3.0	1.78	2.6	1.68	2.4	1.60	2.3
0.79	3	2	4.11	5.2	2.77	3.5	2.50	3.2	2.33	3.0	2.10	2.7	2.02	2.6	1.95	2.5
0.86	2	3	4.40	5.1	3.17	3.7	2.91	3.4	2.72	3.2	2.47	2.9	2.38	2.8	2.31	2.7
1.05	4	2	4.80	4.6	3.13	3.0	2.82	2.7	2.62	2.5	2.36	2.3	2.27	2.2	2.20	2.1
1.21	3	3	5.18	4.3	3.68	3.0	3.38	2.8	3.18	2.6	2.91	2.4	2.81	2.3	2.73	2.3
1.52	4	3	5.87	3.9	4.09	2.7	3.76	2.5	3.52	2.3	3.24	2.1	3.13	2.1	3.05	2.0
1.96	6	3	7.11	3.6	4.74	2.4	4.33	2.2	4.05	2.1	3.69	1.9	3.58	1.8	3.47	1.8
2.16	3	3	7.18	3.3	5.43	2.5	5.15	2.4	4.89	2.3	4.55	2.1	4.46	2.1	4.32	2.0
2.35	5	4	7.56	3.2	5.51	2.3	5.00	2.1	4.74	2.0	4.39	1.9	4.27	1.8	4.17	1.8
2.60	6	4	8.17	3.1	5.74	2.2	5.31	2.0	5.00	1.9	4.63	1.8	4.49	1.7	4.38	1.7
2.95	5	5	8.56	2.9	6.40	2.2	5.94	2.0	5.58	1.9	5.28	1.8	5.15	1.7	5.04	1.7
3.24	6	5	9.22	2.9	6.74	2.1	6.26	1.9	5.95	1.8	5.55	1.7	5.41	1.7	5.29	1.6
3.89	6	6	10.28	2.6	7.72	2.0	7.24	1.9	6.88	1.8	6.46	1.7	6.32	1.6	6.20	1.6
4.16	7	6	10.89	2.6	8.06	1.9	7.50	1.8	7.17	1.7	6.70	1.6	6.55	1.6	6.42	1.5
5.32	9	7	13.28	2.5	9.68	1.8	9.03	1.7	8.60	1.6	8.06	1.5	7.87	1.5	7.72	1.5
6.07	9	8	14.31	2.4	10.68	1.8	10.01	1.7	9.57	1.6	9.02	1.5	8.83	1.5	8.67	1.4
7.04	10	9	16.00	2.3	11.98	1.7	11.25	1.6	10.77	1.5	10.17	1.4	9.96	1.4	9.80	1.4
8.01	11	10	17.69	2.2	13.29	1.7	12.50	1.6	11.98	1.5	11.32	1.4	11.10	1.4	10.91	1.4
9.00	12	11	19.37	2.2	14.59	1.6	13.74	1.5	13.18	1.5	12.47	1.4	12.23	1.4	12.03	1.3
10.00	13	12	21.06	2.1	15.90	1.6	14.98	1.5	14.38	1.4	13.62	1.4	13.37	1.3	13.15	1.3

Table 10 Derivation of Single Sampling Plans

Values of np_1 and c for constructing single sampling plans whose O.C. curve is required to pass through the two points $(p_1, 1 - \alpha)$ and (p_2, β) †.

(Here p_1 is the fraction defective for which the risk of rejection is to be α, and p_2 is the fraction defective for which the risk of acceptance is to be β. To construct the plan, find the tabular value of p_2/p_1 in the column for the given α and β which is equal to or just greater than the given value of the ratio. The sample size is found by dividing the np_1 corresponding to the selected ratio by p_1. The acceptance number is the value of c corresponding to the selected value of the ratio.)

Values of p_2/p_1 for:

c	$\alpha = 0.05$ $\beta = 0.10$	$\alpha = 0.05$ $\beta = 0.05$	$\alpha = 0.05$ $\beta = 0.01$	np_1
0	44.890	58.404	89.781	0.052
1	10.946	13.349	18.681	0.355
2	6.509	7.699	10.280	0.818
3	4.890	5.675	7.352	1.366
4	4.057	4.646	5.890	1.970
5	3.549	4.023	5.017	2.613
6	3.206	3.604	4.435	3.286
7	2.957	3.303	4.019	3.981
8	2.768	3.074	3.707	4.695
9	2.618	2.895	3.462	5.426
10	2.497	2.750	3.265	6.169
11	2.397	2.630	3.104	6.924
12	2.312	2.528	2.968	7.690
13	2.240	2.442	2.852	8.464
14	2.177	2.367	2.752	9.246
15	2.122	2.302	2.665	10.035
16	2.073	2.244	2.588	10.831
17	2.029	2.192	2.520	11.633
18	1.990	2.145	2.458	12.442
19	1.954	2.103	2.403	13.254

Values of p_2/p_1 for:

c	$\alpha = 0.01$ $\beta = 0.10$	$\alpha = 0.01$ $\beta = 0.05$	$\alpha = 0.01$ $\beta = 0.01$	np_1
0	229.105	298.073	458.210	0.010
1	26.184	31.933	44.686	0.149
2	12.206	14.439	19.278	0.436
3	8.115	9.418	12.202	0.823
4	6.249	7.156	9.072	1.279
5	5.195	5.889	7.343	1.785
6	4.520	5.082	6.253	2.330
7	4.050	4.524	5.506	2.906
8	3.705	4.115	4.962	3.507
9	3.440	3.803	4.548	4.130
10	3.229	3.555	4.222	4.771
11	3.058	3.354	3.959	5.428
12	2.915	3.188	3.742	6.099
13	2.795	3.047	3.559	6.782
14	2.692	2.927	3.403	7.477
15	2.603	2.823	3.269	8.181
16	2.524	2.732	3.151	8.895
17	2.455	2.652	3.048	9.616
18	2.393	2.580	2.956	10.346
19	2.337	2.516	2.874	11.082

Table 10 continued Derivation of Single Sampling Plans

| | Values of p_2/p_1 for: $\alpha = 0.05$ | | | | | Values of p_2/p_1 for: $\alpha = 0.01$ | | | |
c	$\beta=0.10$	$\beta=0.05$	$\beta=0.01$	np_1	c	$\beta=0.10$	$\beta=0.05$	$\beta=0.01$	np_1
20	1.922	2.065	2.352	14.072	20	2.287	2.458	2.799	11.825
21	1.892	2.030	2.307	14.894	21	2.241	2.405	2.733	12.574
22	1.865	1.999	2.265	15.719	22	2.200	2.357	2.671	13.329
23	1.840	1.969	2.223	16.548	23	2.162	2.313	2.615	14.088
24	1.817	1.942	2.191	17.382	24	2.126	2.272	2.564	14.853
25	1.795	1.917	2.158	18.218	25	2.094	2.235	2.516	15.623
26	1.775	1.893	2.127	19.058	26	2.064	2.200	2.472	16.397
27	1.757	1.871	2.098	19.900	27	2.035	2.168	2.431	17.175
28	1.739	1.850	2.071	20.746	28	2.009	2.138	2.393	17.957
29	1.723	1.831	2.046	21.594	29	1.985	2.110	2.358	18.742
30	1.707	1.813	2.023	22.444	30	1.962	2.083	2.324	19.532
31	1.692	1.796	2.001	23.298	31	1.940	2.059	2.293	20.324
32	1.679	1.780	1.980	24.152	32	1.920	2.035	2.264	21.120
33	1.665	1.764	1.960	25.010	33	1.900	2.013	2.236	21.919
34	1.653	1.750	1.941	25.870	34	1.882	1.992	2.210	22.721
35	1.641	1.736	1.923	26.731	35	1.865	1.973	2.185	23.525
36	1.630	1.723	1.906	27.594	36	1.848	1.954	2.162	24.333
37	1.619	1.710	1.890	28.460	37	1.833	1.936	2.139	25.143
38	1.609	1.698	1.875	29.327	38	1.818	1.920	2.118	25.955
39	1.599	1.687	1.860	30.196	39	1.804	1.903	2.098	26.770
40	1.590	1.676	1.846	31.066	40	1.790	1.887	2.079	27.587
41	1.581	1.666	1.833	31.938	41	1.777	1.873	2.060	28.406
42	1.572	1.656	1.820	32.812	42	1.765	1.859	2.043	29.228
43	1.564	1.646	1.807	33.686	43	1.753	1.845	2.026	30.051
44	1.556	1.637	1.796	34.563	44	1.742	1.832	2.010	30.877
45	1.548	1.628	1.784	35.441	45	1.731	1.820	1.994	31.704
46	1.541	1.619	1.773	36.320	46	1.720	1.808	1.980	32.534
47	1.534	1.611	1.763	37.200	47	1.710	1.796	1.965	33.365
48	1.527	1.603	1.752	38.082	48	1.701	1.785	1.952	34.198
49	1.521	1.596	1.743	38.965	49	1.691	1.775	1.938	35.032

† Reprinted by permission from J. M. Cameron. 'Tables for Constructing and for Computing the Operating Characteristics of Single-Sampling Plans', *Industrial Quality Control*, July 1952, pp. 37–39.

Table 11 Construction of O.C. Curves for Single Sampling Plans

Values of np_1 for which the probability of acceptance of c or fewer defectives in a sample of n is $P(A)$†.

(To find the fraction defective p, corresponding to a probability of acceptance $P(A)$ in a single sampling plan with sample size n and acceptance number c, divide by n the entry in the row for the given c and the column for the given $P(A)$.)

$P(A) =$	0.995	0.990	0.975	0.950	0.900	0.750	0.500	0.250	0.100	0.050	0.025	0.010	0.005
$c=0$	0.00501	0.0101	0.0253	0.0513	0.105	0.288	0.693	1.386	2.303	2.996	3.689	4.605	5.298
1	0.103	0.149	0.242	0.355	0.532	0.961	1.678	2.693	3.890	4.744	5.572	6.638	7.430
2	0.338	0.436	0.619	0.818	1.102	1.727	2.674	3.920	5.322	6.296	7.224	8.406	9.274
3	0.672	0.823	1.090	1.366	1.745	2.535	3.672	5.109	6.681	7.754	8.768	10.045	10.978
4	1.078	1.279	1.623	1.970	2.433	3.369	4.671	6.274	7.994	9.154	10.242	11.605	12.594
5	1.537	1.785	2.202	2.613	3.152	4.219	5.670	7.423	9.275	10.513	11.668	13.108	14.150
6	2.037	2.330	2.814	3.286	3.895	5.083	6.670	8.558	10.532	11.842	13.060	14.571	15.660
7	2.571	2.906	3.454	3.981	4.656	5.956	7.669	9.684	11.771	13.148	14.422	16.000	17.134
8	3.132	3.507	4.115	4.695	5.432	6.838	8.669	10.802	12.995	14.434	15.763	17.403	18.578
9	3.717	4.130	4.795	5.426	6.221	7.726	9.669	11.914	14.206	15.705	17.085	18.783	19.998
10	4.321	4.771	5.491	6.169	7.021	8.620	10.668	13.020	15.407	16.962	18.390	20.145	21.398
11	4.943	5.428	6.201	6.924	7.829	9.519	11.668	14.121	16.598	18.208	19.682	21.490	22.779
12	5.580	6.099	6.922	7.690	8.646	10.422	12.668	15.217	17.782	19.442	20.962	22.821	24.145
13	6.231	6.782	7.654	8.464	9.470	11.329	13.668	16.310	18.958	20.668	22.230	24.139	25.496
14	6.893	7.477	8.396	9.246	10.300	12.239	14.668	17.400	20.128	21.886	23.490	25.446	26.836
15	7.566	8.181	9.144	10.035	11.135	13.152	15.668	18.486	21.292	23.098	24.741	26.743	28.166
16	8.249	8.895	9.902	10.831	11.976	14.068	16.668	19.570	22.452	24.302	25.984	28.031	29.484
17	8.942	9.616	10.666	11.633	12.822	14.986	17.668	20.652	23.606	25.500	27.220	29.310	30.792
18	9.644	10.346	11.438	12.442	13.672	15.907	18.668	21.731	24.756	26.692	28.448	30.581	32.092
19	10.353	11.082	12.216	13.254	14.525	16.830	19.668	22.808	25.902	27.879	29.671	31.845	33.383

Table 11 continued Construction of O.C. Curves for Single Sampling Plans

20	11.069	11.825	12.999	14.072	15.383	17.755	20.668	23.883	27.045	29.062	30.888	33.103	34.668
21	11.791	12.574	13.787	14.894	16.244	18.682	21.668	24.956	28.184	30.241	32.102	34.355	35.947
22	12.520	13.329	14.580	15.719	17.108	19.610	22.668	26.028	29.320	31.416	33.309	35.601	37.219
23	13.255	14.088	15.377	16.548	17.975	20.540	23.668	27.098	30.453	32.586	34.512	36.841	38.485
24	13.995	14.853	16.178	17.382	18.844	21.471	24.668	28.167	31.584	33.752	35.710	38.077	39.745
25	14.740	15.623	16.984	18.218	19.717	22.404	25.667	29.234	32.711	34.916	36.905	39.308	41.000
26	15.490	16.397	17.793	19.058	20.592	23.338	26.667	30.300	33.836	36.077	38.096	40.535	42.252
27	16.245	17.175	18.606	19.900	21.469	24.273	27.667	31.365	34.959	37.234	39.284	41.757	43.497
28	17.004	17.957	19.422	20.746	22.348	25.209	28.667	32.428	36.080	38.389	40.468	42.975	44.738
29	17.767	18.742	20.241	21.594	23.229	26.147	29.667	33.491	37.198	39.541	41.649	44.190	45.976
30	18.534	19.532	21.063	22.444	24.113	27.086	30.667	34.552	38.315	40.690	42.827	45.401	47.210
31	19.305	20.324	21.888	23.298	24.998	28.025	31.667	35.613	39.430	41.838	44.002	46.609	48.440
32	20.079	21.120	22.716	24.152	25.885	28.966	32.667	36.672	40.543	42.982	45.174	47.813	49.666
33	20.856	21.919	23.546	25.010	26.774	29.907	33.667	37.731	41.654	44.125	46.344	49.015	50.888
34	21.638	22.721	24.379	25.870	27.664	30.849	34.667	38.788	42.764	45.266	47.512	50.213	52.108
35	22.422	23.525	25.214	26.731	28.556	31.792	35.667	39.845	43.872	46.404	48.676	51.409	53.324
36	23.208	24.333	26.052	27.594	29.450	32.736	36.667	40.901	44.978	47.540	49.840	52.601	54.538
37	23.998	25.143	26.891	28.460	30.345	33.681	37.667	41.957	46.083	48.676	51.000	53.791	55.748
38	24.791	25.955	27.733	29.327	31.241	34.626	38.667	43.011	47.187	49.808	52.158	54.979	56.956
39	25.586	26.770	28.576	30.196	32.139	35.572	39.667	44.065	48.289	50.940	53.314	56.164	58.160
40	26.384	27.587	29.422	31.066	33.038	36.519	40.667	45.118	49.390	52.069	54.469	57.347	59.363
41	27.184	28.406	30.270	31.938	33.938	37.466	41.667	46.171	50.490	53.197	55.622	58.528	60.563
42	27.986	29.228	31.120	32.812	34.839	38.414	42.667	47.223	51.589	54.324	56.772	59.717	61.761
43	28.791	30.051	31.970	33.686	35.742	39.363	43.667	48.274	52.686	55.449	57.921	60.884	62.956
44	29.598	30.877	32.824	34.563	36.646	40.312	44.667	49.325	53.782	56.572	59.068	62.059	64.150
45	30.408	31.704	33.678	35.441	37.550	41.262	45.667	50.375	54.878	57.695	60.214	63.231	65.340
46	31.219	32.534	34.534	36.320	38.456	42.212	46.667	51.425	55.972	58.816	61.358	64.402	66.529
47	32.032	33.365	35.392	37.200	39.363	43.163	47.667	52.474	57.065	59.936	62.500	65.571	67.716
48	32.848	34.198	36.250	38.082	40.270	44.115	48.667	53.522	58.158	61.054	63.641	66.738	68.901
49	33.664	35.032	37.111	38.965	41.179	45.067	49.667	54.571	59.249	62.171	64.780	67.903	70.084

†Reprinted by permission from J. M. Cameron. 'Tables for Constructing and for Computing the Operating Characteristics of Single-Sampling Plans', *Industrial Quality Control*, July 1952, pp. 37–39.

Index